Increase Reading Volume

Increase Reading Volume

Practical Strategies That Boost Students' Achievement and Passion for Reading

Laura Robb

NCTE
National Council of Teachers of English
340 N. Neil St., Suite #104, Champaign, Illinois 61820
www.ncte.org

Staff Editors: Kurt Austin and Cynthia Gomez
Manuscript Editor: Michael Ryan
Interior Design: Jenny Jensen Greenleaf
Cover Design: Pat Mayer

ISBN 978-0-8141-5195-2 (paperback); ISBN 978-0-8141-5197-6 (ebook)

It is the policy of NCTE in its journals and other publications to provide a forum for the open discussion of ideas concerning the content and the teaching of English and the language arts. Publicity accorded to any particular point of view does not imply endorsement by the Executive Committee, the Board of Directors, or the membership at large, except in announcements of policy, where such endorsement is clearly specified.

NCTE provides equal employment opportunity to all staff members and applicants for employment without regard to race, color, religion, sex, national origin, age, physical, mental or perceived handicap/disability, sexual orientation including gender identity or expression, ancestry, genetic information, marital status, military status, unfavorable discharge from military service, pregnancy, citizenship status, personal appearance, matriculation or political affiliation, or any other protected status under applicable federal, state, and local laws.

Every effort has been made to provide current URLs and email addresses, but, because of the rapidly changing nature of the web, some sites and addresses may no longer be accessible.

Library of Congress Control Number: 2022948418

With love for my grandson, Lucas, who loves to read and has a rich, personal reading life. Through our conversations about books, you have opened my mind to new topics and genres and increased my curiosity—and for that, I am eternally grateful!

Contents

FOREWORD ... ix
JIM BURKE

PREFACE: MY READING TEACHER LIFE TURNS UPSIDE DOWN ... xiii

ACKNOWLEDGMENTS ... xvii

CHAPTER 1 Engagement Leads to Volume in Reading ... 1

CHAPTER 2 Teaching with Intentionality ... 16

CHAPTER 3 The Importance of Independent Reading ... 34

CHAPTER 4 Extending the Reach of Partner and Small-Group Collaborations ... 54

CHAPTER 5 Increase Reading Volume: Instructional Reading Unit Libraries ... 73

CHAPTER 6 Core Collections—Core Text and Related Contemporary Texts ... 99

CHAPTER 7 Suggestions for Getting Started and Moving Forward ... 118

APPENDIXES 125

WORKS CITED 145

INDEX 153

AUTHOR 159

Foreword

JIM BURKE, *Middle College High School, San Mateo, CA*
Author of The English Teacher's Companion *and editor of* Uncharted Territory, *2nd ed.*

Last year, I decided to subscribe to MasterClass, the series of high-quality seminars featuring the Great Ones who have distinguished themselves as chefs, designers, writers, leaders, and much more. Imagine the pleasure and practical value of listening to a series of short talks by Malcolm Gladwell about how to write great nonfiction or Salman Rushdie on how stories work. Imagine the insights and intelligence about diplomacy that the MasterClass taught by Madeleine Albright and Condoleezza Rice offers to those who make a little time each day to sit down, listen to, and learn from such masters of their craft.

This is what it was like for me to read this book by Laura Robb.

Over the course of my teaching career, few things have been as steady as the challenge to help my high school students become confident, willing, independent readers who can find their own books (or other texts) and maintain the attentional stamina and engagement needed to enjoy reading or, when necessary, persevere through those texts that may not be fun but are important to be able to make sense of within the larger context of their learning.

To these challenges, which are certainly enough on their own, we would have to add the challenge of helping students develop and maintain an identity of themselves *as* readers, as the sort of people who can and *do* read for a range of purposes, including for pleasure. These challenges have been real and persistent whether I was teaching freshman "remedial English," as it was called when I first began teaching over thirty years ago, seniors in AP English literature, or my current students at Middle College High School, located on a two-year college campus where they are in my high school English class for one hour before running across campus to attend a college philosophy, biology, or psychology class where the volume and complexity of the reading demands are intense.

As I read Laura's book, I felt like she was responding in 2022, guided by her vast experience, wisdom, and the latest research, to questions I have grappled with since I began teaching in 1989. For while I may have made progress when it comes to teaching and engaging my students as readers, the truth is that we are competing in what some describe as an "attention economy," that attention being a very limited resource for which the competition is fierce.

Throughout this book you are holding, we learn a remarkable number and range of strategies to help secondary students improve their stamina and become more engaged, independent readers, thanks to Laura's many suggestions in these areas. What stays with me after reading this book, however, is that you cannot turn a page without learning what it means to be a fully engaged teacher of reading, for on each page you learn not only what Laura does to engage readers or teach students how to find books they will want to read, but you learn *how* she does it, how she *thinks* about such interactions between students and their teachers, between students and each other, between readers and the texts they read. It is in these ways that this book is a MasterClass with one of the most thoughtful, passionate, and dedicated teacher-leaders in our profession. As a teacher of reading (and how to write about and discuss it in class or individual conferences), Laura Robb embodies Henry James's admonition that we should strive to be "one on whom nothing is lost" when it comes to reading and how to teach it.

This is a book that is not only filled with what Laura has learned throughout her long and distinguished career but is packed with all that the changes in our society and schools have forced us to learn to do and consider if our classes are to be culturally responsive, equitable, and engaging to everyone. We all know that we should be having students write about and discuss different types of texts, but most of us struggle to know what that looks like and how to implement such practices in ways that make the intended difference. In this brief but substantive book, Laura Robb, as her work has done for years, reminds us that to be a teacher of reading, to instill in our students a love of reading, to cultivate an environment that embraces literacy in our classrooms, cannot happen in isolation nor by accident. It requires intentionality and the support of administrators and other leaders, for as Laura writes here, "positive changes are more likely to occur in a school where the principal and other administrators continually build trusting relationships among staff, encourage teacher leadership and feedback, and set aside time to have ongoing conversations" about literacy in general as the connection to privilege, racism, and deficit models (19).

Fundamental to this mission of individual and institutional change in literacy is Laura's own example, both to us and to her students, of how reading shapes both her personal *and* professional life. This connection and commitment is evident when she writes:

> Yes, it's important to read and know the literature that relates to the content you teach; that's a given. But it's also important for you to carve out time to develop your own reading life, for doing this enables you to talk to students about recent books you enjoyed. It also enlarges your understanding of the value of volume in reading: building vocabulary, improving recall and comprehension, and developing a clearer understanding of a specific text structure. The more you connect to yourself as a reader, the better able you are to make connections with and for students. For example, when [one of my students] Oscar told me during a conference, "When I read on my own, I like graphic novels; I can stick with it and get into the story."
>
> I was able to reply, "You know, I like to read magazines and mysteries on my own because even if I'm tired, I can read them. It's okay to read books that are pure fun."
>
> Oscar looked befuddled at first, and then said, "Yeah. I'm... I'm reading..."
>
> "That's what counts," I told him.
>
> And Oscar grinned.
>
> A personal reading life enables you to experience the power of visualizing as a path to understanding, the need to talk to someone about a book resonating with you, and that sometimes, reading can be challenging work. Your enthusiasm for and engagement in reading can rub off on students as they choose books they want to and can read, ensuring they will be engaged. (13–14)

Though this book is short, it is built on a solid foundation of established and current research, combined with Laura's own experiences in the classroom, where she continues to work with kids of all backgrounds and grade levels.

Returning to the MasterClass series of seminars I mentioned at the beginning, I appreciate the way I can choose to read and use this gem of a book to help me think about what to teach with a particular text, how to teach it, how I might have students write about, discuss, or respond to it, and how I might go about assessing their understanding throughout the reading of that text. As with those MasterClass seminars, I can jump in and listen to Malcolm Gladwell talk for fifteen fascinating minutes about just the importance of titles, or I can settle in and let Malcolm tell me in much greater detail about how he thinks and works as a master craftsman of nonfiction. So it is here with Laura Robb: I can dip in for ten or fifteen minutes for a MasterClass-like seminar about using class discussion to improve engagement, or I can settle in and read a whole chapter about how to pair core texts and more contemporary, culturally relevant titles.

As she does with her own students, regardless of what she is teaching, Laura Robb is going to always make us feel that we can do for ourselves what she is here to help us do for all of our students:

Every student in your class deserves to improve their reading expertise and develop a personal reading life. This will most likely occur when you increase students' volume in reading, discussions about books, and writing about reading in notebooks. In addition, during frequent conferences, encourage reflection on their reading progress and how books have changed their thinking. With your support and understanding of students' needs, reading can become a positive, lifelong experience that enables students to be analytical, think critically, problem solve, and best of all, read to learn and for pleasure! (123)

Preface

My Reading Teacher Life Turns Upside Down

"I hate reading."
"You'll never make me like reading."
"Boring!"
"[Reading] makes me sleepy."
"Books are just words. Lots of 'em."

These comments are from middle grade and middle school students reading three or more years below grade level, responding to the question I ask each one during a conference: *How do you feel about reading?* Like me, at first, you might bristle when you hear their words because you and I always hope that students will love reading. Moreover, these responses can increase personal anxieties and feelings of being unprepared to meet such teaching challenges. Despite our best efforts, many children in our care don't feel a connection to books, and for those children, reading is hard work that makes them tired—it's work they try to avoid.

While anxiety and frustration are understandable in a listener, it's important to move beyond both and credit students with being honest, even if that honesty reveals their own anger and frustration. Whether in elementary, middle, or high school, students frequently have difficulty finding the words to ask, *Can you help me be a better reader?* But that's the message these developing readers—students reading three or more years below grade level—are telegraphing when they use *hate* and *boring* to describe their feelings toward reading.

How can we best serve these students?

This question continually replayed in my mind and the minds of the fifth- and sixth-grade teachers who I coach in Winchester, Virginia. As we searched for answers, one thought from my past experiences continually pummeled my mind: choosing to read books at school and at home increases volume in reading—and research shows a strong correlation between reading volume and students' growth as readers (Allington and McGill-Franzen 2021). Daily reading at school not only increases volume, but it also provides the practice these students need to improve comprehension and develop a personal reading life. However, progress is not as simple as finding time for developing readers to read every day, and so my teaching life turned upside down. To learn more about these developing readers, teachers and I held frequent short conferences.

Conferring pointed out that these students carried emotional baggage. For example, during past experiences with round-robin reading, some of their peers snickered when these students stumbled over words they couldn't decode, causing them to retreat into a silent, cooperative stance, hoping no one would call on them. Reviewing three consecutive years of state testing in reading and vocabulary revealed a steady decline in their scores. Not surprising—they weren't reading, and many had difficulty decoding. The teachers and I agreed that before inviting students to choose books they could read and find a comfortable place to read them, we had to help students feel safe by:

- Honoring their language and encouraging translanguaging during discussions and when they wrote about reading in their notebooks.
- Explaining that drawing was writing and that they could use pictures in their responses to reading.
- Assuring them repeatedly that they would *not* be asked to read aloud during class and making good on this promise.
- Showing them that reading "easy" books was okay and explaining that as they read and practiced reading, they would improve.
- Modeling again and again how to choose a "good fit" book.
- Listening to their fears and hopes about reading during conferences and, with their help, finding ways to support them.
- Integrating word sorting and word study into lessons to improve decoding skills and develop their knowledge of phonics and how our language works.

Progress among students didn't occur quickly. The poet Eve Merriam said, "It takes a lot of slow to grow," and we learned that it wasn't possible to rush children forward. Teachers and I followed students' lead and had daily conversations that became reminders of the importance to teach the children in front of us instead of covering curriculum.

An Asset Model

An asset model focuses on what students can do. When you base instructional decisions on students' strengths, interests, and desires to learn, and you also show students' that you value their assets and potential and are willing to build trusting relationships with them, then it's possible to help students become readers. To support students' reading progress, teachers and I identified six areas that continually require attention whether they are developing, proficient, or advanced readers.

Use time strategically. If you're having difficulty including independent reading of self-selected books at the end of class, move it to the first thing your students do. Whether you have forty or sixty minutes for reading, make independent and instructional reading priorities. With forty to forty-five-minute periods, plan over two weeks: three days for reading and two for writing the first week and three days for writing and two for reading the second week.

Increase reading volume. When students read self-selected books daily, they develop the habit of independent reading and soon choose to read at home for pleasure. Increased volume enlarges students' vocabularies and can create lifelong readers who turn to books to learn and to enjoy.

Build students' vocabulary and background knowledge through daily teacher read-alouds and short videos that increase students' background knowledge of genres and topics, enabling them to connect to books on diverse topics.

Practice decoding words, developing fluency, and studying word families and completing word sorts; they all contribute to students' abilities to read expressively and with understanding. Students can complete word sorts, build word families, and for increasing fluency, practice reading and rereading poems that they volunteer to perform.

Improve comprehension. This occurs when students choose and can read texts to discuss with partners and in small groups as well as when they respond to open-ended questions that have more than one answer and can support their answers with text evidence. These conversations combined with writing about reading also develop students' critical thinking and ability to connect ideas.

Using formative assessments includes careful teacher observations of students as they work and conferring with students to discuss texts and explore their evolving reading attitudes. In addition, the writing about reading that students complete in their notebooks can reveal their level of comprehension and ability to use vocabulary related to a text and unit.

In *Increase Reading Volume*, I'm not offering scripts and recipes; I already know—and research corroborates this statement—that you, the teacher, are the key to your students' learning and progress. I know that you can and will adapt and adjust the ideas in this book to what *your students* show you they need. Though you and I may live far apart, this book allows us to work together with the goal of developing all students' personal reading lives.

My experiences learning with developing readers imprinted this thought in my mind: *Volume in reading matters to the reading growth and pleasure in reading of developing, proficient, and advanced readers!* I look forward to doing this work with you and your colleagues in the pages that follow.

Acknowledgments

First, I'd like to thank Robb Clouse, who encouraged me to write this book for NCTE, and Kurt Austin, for ushering the book through the process of peer review and editing. It is a topic that Richard Allington, Stephen Krashen, Mary Howard, and I have championed. And to my students, those who hated reading and those who embraced reading: you led me to reflect on ways to increase reading volume in middle school and high school—and I thank you for your suggestions and honesty! You also validated my belief that having choices, reflecting on, discussing, and writing about reading can develop a deeper understanding of texts and enhance readers' ability to think critically and to connect and evaluate ideas.

Deep thanks to my son Evan Robb, principal of Johnson Williams Middle School, for reading early and revised drafts of the book. You always offered helpful feedback that led me to rethink ideas and revise content. Thanks, too, for the wonderful essay you wrote from the principal's perspective and for the tips it includes. Thanks to Bridget Wilson and Wanda Waters for their work using instructional genre-based reading units, giving students choices, and providing me with excellent feedback. Finally, to all the teachers I've coached and learned with, my sincere thanks! You have embraced volume in reading and understand the value of students' self-selecting books for independent and instructional reading. You are the change makers who recognize that for students to become readers, they need access to the finest, culturally relevant books!

Note: All names of teachers and students are pseudonyms with the exception of Bridget Wilson, Wanda Waters, and Evan Robb.

1

Engagement Leads to Volume in Reading

"What kind of teaching is this, anyway?" and "You're weird, lady. What're we gonna learn from you reading to us? This is dumb!" These comments made by seventh and eighth graders as they rushed out of my first class with them were not exactly what I had hoped for. The sixteen students had been handpicked by teachers to work with me every day for forty-five minutes. Teachers believed these students should be succeeding in English class, but after years of not reading at school and/or at home, they lacked stamina, a rich reading vocabulary, and background knowledge. Skill and drill worksheets and reading cards with short text and five multiple-choice questions were the backbone of their "remedial" program. It wasn't working. The principal and the superintendent wanted change.

Though it was several years ago, I still recall sitting opposite Mary Ann Biggs, principal of Johnson Williams Middle School in Berryville, Virginia, and Dennis Kellison, superintendent of Clarke County Schools. Both wanted to know if they hired me, what type of reading curriculum I would offer these students. I outlined a curriculum based on *The Meaning Makers* by Gordon Wells (1985). Wells conducted extensive research and showed that stories and storying are central to all learning. In fact, stories have a role in education far beyond the acquisition of literacy, and storying—the telling of stories we tell ourselves to connect past experiences to new knowledge—is the way human beings learn across disciplines. I proposed a reading workshop that included daily teacher read-alouds, responding to my read-alouds through discussion and shared writing, and independent reading of self-selected books. We agreed there would be no grades or tests because the primary goal was to bring students into the reading life. Two weeks before school started, Mrs. Biggs sent a letter home to parents, explaining the goals of this extra reading class.

During the first six classes, I read short stories, ones I considered action packed and filled with suspense. Frontloading activities were unsuccessful; no one participated. The suspense and tension of "The Elevator" by William Sleator (1989) did not appear to interest the students. My eyes scanned the group as

I read. Billy's head was on his desk, his eyes closed. Four students were drawing in notebooks. The rest slumped in their chairs, disinterested, disconnected, and disengaged.

The first story that caught students' attention was *Captain Murderer* by Charles Dickens, as retold by George Harland. The bloodthirsty, cannibalistic captain, who murdered his beautiful young brides on their wedding night and then baked them in a pie crust before eating this hearty dinner, had them at the edge of their seats. "Read it again," said three different voices. And as I began the story again, I rejoiced inwardly at these reactions.

The next class included a discussion of *Captain Murderer*. "Gruesome, gory, great" were some initial comments I recorded on chart paper. "He eats humans. Isn't there a word for that?" asked Richard.

I printed *cannibalism* on the chart and Jack added, "Yeah. That's the word."

Then I asked the class, "How do you feel about the last bride sacrificing herself to destroy the captain?' Silence. "Turn-and talk, and then you can share." Silence.

Then Chip blurted out, "That lady was dumb to give up her life."

"Yeah," said Jack. "She coulda thought of something else."

"But she didn't," said Casey. "Sometimes you gotta help others."

The discussion continued until the bell rang, and the class filed out, some students still arguing about the bride's decision. This was the first real discussion among them, the first time I observed them involved with a story and sharing how they felt and thought.

Armed with a small success, I decided to read aloud *The Great Gilly Hopkins* (by Katherine Paterson) next, as I believed that Gilly's anger and dysfunction would resonate with these students. I reserved the remaining thirty minutes of class time for independent reading of self-selected books. During short conferences when I asked each student, "How can you become a better reader?" ten answered, "By reading—I guess." The rest told me, "That's your job."

Up to this point, not one student had noticed the shelves at the back of the room filled with hundreds of books or wondered why the books were there. I forced myself to have no expectations when I introduced the classroom library and modeled how to choose a book. Choice did not immediately motivate students to read; however, after several weeks of modeling how to choose a book, most were able to find a "good fit" book and a comfortable place to read. The day Richard and Keysha objected to the bell ringing, marking the end of independent reading, was a milestone moment. One-on-one conferences also revealed students' change of heart toward reading, and many asked me to add more adventure and fantasy books to their classroom library. And I did, believing that to make the library theirs, students needed to have input on new additions, so the library included books they desired to read.

Why I Shared This Literacy Snapshot

Throughout my teaching life, my students have been my teachers. Sure, I learn from reading professional books and articles, visiting classrooms, attending conferences, and having conversations with colleagues. However, when I step into the classroom, I learn from students how I might support them and not judge their feelings about reading. I learn to be patient and to say nothing negative when I offer them two to three books to browse through, and they return them to a shelf. I learn how important choice is and that abandoning a book is okay, as I don't want them to read a book that doesn't engage and interest them. I learn to notice every millimeter of progress each one makes and to share it during a conference or as I high-five students exiting the class. Wanting them to experience the joys of reading is important to me, but I quickly understand that it's best to put my agenda in the deep freeze and let them find their own way into reading. And this happens at different points during the year.

By spring, most students increased their stamina and could read for twenty to thirty minutes during independent reading. When two students ask to check out a book and take it home, I notice that each day, a few more ask. Having a rich, diverse classroom library and time to read at school shows students how much I value reading. Moreover, reading self-selected books at school every day develops a pleasurable habit that students frequently transfer to at-home reading. I watch with delight their reading odometers collect reading mileage.

Volume in reading and time to read books relevant to their lives and the world improves their vocabulary and enlarges their background knowledge. A culturally relevant classroom library offers easy access to books, and time to settle down and read every day increases the amount of books students complete. Setting aside time for pairs of students and small groups to discuss books they enjoy and those they abandon offers students possible books to investigate and maybe read. Over time, resisting reading and "I hate reading" comments can diminish. Though elementary school teachers have the time in their schedules for students to read for pleasure, most middle and high school teachers don't. Research reveals that by middle school, the amount of time students read independently at school decreases and remains on this trajectory through high school (Scholastic 2019).

Studies Show Our Students Aren't Reading Enough

Scholastic continues to conduct studies of the amount of reading students do at school and at home. Their results correlate with the flat trend in reading scores on our nation's report card, the National Assessment for Educational Progress (NAEP), from 2009–2019.

- Daily in-school independent reading occurs for 17 percent of students ages six to seventeen (Scholastic 2015).
- By age nine, reading volume starts to drop: 35 percent of nine-year-old children report reading five to seven days a week compared to 57 percent of eight-year-old children (Scholastic 2019).
- Since 2009, there has been a steady decline of children reading nearly every day, and a rise in those reading less than one day a week (Scholastic 2019).
- Survey findings based on nearly 3,700 preK–12 teachers and principals show that 94 percent of principals and teachers agree or strongly agree that students should choose books at school and read independently every day, but only 36 percent made time for daily independent reading (Scholastic 2017).

This continual drop in time students read independently at school can have a negative effect on children's literacy development and ultimately result in disengagement with reading due to a lack of daily practice (Allington 1977, 2011, 2013; Goldberg and Houser 2020; Miller and Sharp 2018; Robb and Robb 2020). Access to books and time to read at school every day that classes meet can foster engagement with reading, increase volume in reading, and can lead to developing a lifelong personal reading journey.

The Seven Pillars of Engagement

These seven pillars work together much like an orchestra does to create the engagement students need in order to read widely and frequently. If the pillars are in place in a school, it reveals that teachers have cultivated the seven because teachers respect students' stories and cultures and strive to be responsive to each reader's unique needs.

1. Choice empowers students to decide which books they want to read or whether to abandon a book and search for a different one. Students' choices develop literary tastes as students discover the authors and genres they enjoy, invest in their reading, and advertise books they love by sharing them with peers. Students become engaged readers when they can choose books to read, set how much time they'll invest in reading, and develop responsibility as they read to meet personal goals and teachers' expectations.

2. **Agency** is an outgrowth of choice, freedom, self-regulated learning, and making decisions. When students take an active role in their education and have autonomy, they can set deadline dates to complete tasks, create learning goals, decide on actions they'll take to reach specific goals, self-evaluate outcomes, and become engaged learners. Ownership is key to agency and often leads to a growth mindset, the belief that with hard work and teacher support, students begin to view mistakes as positive information to learn from and use to move forward (Dweck 2007).

3. **Relationships** between teacher and student in school or during virtual learning can lead to positive interactions and create a thriving community of engaged learners. Teachers who invest in relationship building throughout the school year ensure that every student feels valued, heard, and respected. To form relationships, be a good listener, take the time to get to know every student as a unique person, honor and enjoy their stories, and share some of yours. Always be approachable, show you care by responding to needs, questions, worries, and joyful moments. When students have positive relationships with teachers and other adults in their schools, they feel part of the community and start to invest in their learning.

4. **Trust** is an important component of building a community of engaged learners and benefits principals, teachers, and students. As principals and teachers collaborate to develop relational trust, improve instruction, and cultivate culturally relevant teaching, students come to trust their teachers and peers and feel confident that both groups will keep them physically and emotionally safe.

5. **Sanctuary** is a safe place. When students learn in schools that are sanctuaries, teachers help them understand that mistakes and failures are part of the learning process. In classrooms that are sanctuaries, students feel valued and have a respect for one another that fosters inclusion over exclusion and tak-

Culturally Relevant Teaching

Culturally relevant teaching asks teachers to view students' native language, history, and families as valuable assets. Teachers can foster engagement by encouraging students to leverage their cultural capital and use their knowledge and unique experiences to support how they learn. This can include translanguaging, inviting students to integrate their primary language into their speaking and writing, and asking parents to provide feedback about how their child learns and what kinds of support might benefit their child (Espana and Herrera 2020; Osorio 2020). In addition, choosing culturally and linguistically sustaining books for teaching counterstories (to white-privileged texts) can deepen students' understanding of social justice in the context of historically accurate texts (Muhammad 2020).

ing risks over compliance. Engagement in learning can flourish when students feel safe and the class community respects their choices, feelings, and thinking.

6. Honest Communication between students and their teacher during conferring, in informal conversations, and in written notes can occur as soon as students feel safe and have a trusting relationship with teachers. When students share their feelings, explanations for behaviors and attitudes, hopes, and dreams, teachers can offer the emotional and academic support that can lead to engagement with reading and learning.

7. Reflection asks students to look back and think about their reading and learning to gain insights about their process that can help them move forward. By cultivating self-awareness, students take responsibility for their learning and explore ways they can grow and improve as critical thinkers. When teachers discuss the benefits of reflection and reserve time for students to revisit reading conversations, choices, and writing about reading, engagement and motivation can increase.

In classrooms where the seven pillars of engagement thrive, the pillars work together and nurture the engagement in reading that students need in order to grow their reading identities and at the same time strengthen their skill through volume in reading.

Engagement Increases Volume in Reading

In 2008, William Brozo, Gerry Shiel, and Keith Topping wrote "Engagement in Reading: Lessons Learned from Three PISA Countries." Using PISA (Program for International Student Assessment) results of the fifteen-year-old students who took the reading test in the United States, the United Kingdom, and the Republic of Ireland, the authors published their findings in ILA's *Journal of Adolescent & Adult Literacy*.

PISA defines literacy as "the capacity of students to apply knowledge and skills and to analyze, reason, and communicate effectively as they pose, solve, and interpret problems in a variety of situations" (305). The PISA test's variable that received the most scrutiny was reading engagement. The authors identified three areas that combined to create engagement in reading and resulted in students reading and enjoying a variety of texts for long periods of time:

- **Diversity of Reading:** Students who often read six types of texts—magazines, comics, fiction books, nonfiction books, email, and webpages.
- **Frequency of Leisure (Independent) Reading:** The amount of time students read self-selected books every day on their own.

- **Attitudes toward Reading:** The reasons why students read are important and statements such as *It's what I love to do; I can get lost in a book and forget the passing of time,* etc., reveal a positive and enthusiastic outlook.

When these three areas work in concert, students continually experience engaged reading and increase their volume. Adolescents engaged in their reading also scored higher on the NAEP (National Assessment of Educational Progress), the nation's report card, and state reading tests. Engaged readers also had better grades in high school than those who were less engaged with reading. In her book *Engaging Children: Igniting a Drive for Deeper Learning K–8*, Ellin Keene shares a chart of visible and invisible conditions in classrooms that lead to student engagement (2018). To encourage reading, Keene notes:

> Teachers encourage children to choose most books and topics for writing and inquiry themselves and make it possible for them to pursue topics of passionate interest—they have equal access to all materials, not just those at their "level." (38)

Keene's respect for learners and her faith in their ability to make choices that work, as well as having the freedom to read without being boxed into "levels," allows students to pursue their passions and set challenging goals. Take seventh grader Helena, who in the primary grades struggled with learning to read but by seventh grade is reading and enjoying books like *The Giver* and *A Long Walk to Water.* One day, she arrives at school with a copy of *To Kill a Mockingbird*. Her teacher tells Helena that she will read it in ninth grade and that she might find the book a challenge. Helena's reply is what I hope all students have the confidence to say: "I've heard from my brother and his friends that it's a great book, so I'll read it now and then read it again in ninth grade."

After rereading parts of the introduction to understand it, Helena read the book and loved it. Sure, she reread parts to "get it." But her desire and passion demonstrate it's possible to push "levels" aside when students have the desire to read long books and willingly reread parts. Reading long books develops students' ability to hold information they learn in early chapters in their memory and then use those details later on in the text when they need to understand an event, decision, conflict, or problem.

When you know students' level of background knowledge on a topic, their reading habits, and the amount of independent reading they're doing, honor their grit and desire by encouraging them to "give a challenging book a go." Check in frequently with the student. Listen. Support. And if the student chooses to stop reading the book, help make that a positive decision.

Volume in Reading Matters

Volume in reading depends on the amount of time students spend reading at school each day and the number of books completed. Amount of books can be tricky because the length of a book is also important. So, if the established number of independent reading books students must read each year is thirty-five to forty-five, it's important to pause and consider what these numbers mean. A seventh grader reads the *Encyclopedia Brown* series, which averages about 100 pages per book, while a student in the same class reads *The Hunger Games* series, which have about 400 pages per book. Students reading longer and more complex books might not reach the required number of books a teacher or school has established. Perhaps it's better to be flexible and accept fewer books from students reading and enjoying longer texts and look at volume in reading from a different angle: the amount of time students read each day.

For students to improve their reading skill, they have to do the reading.

When you or your students ask, *Why can't I skip twenty minutes of independent reading homework today or for several days?*, the research of Anderson, Wilson, and Fielding (1988) tells the story. Their study found a correlation between the time students devote to daily reading and their reading proficiency and comprehension scores.

> In sum, the principal conclusion of this study is that the amount of time a child spends reading books is related to the child's reading level in the fifth grade and growth in reading proficiency from second to fifth grade. The case can be made that reading books is a cause, not merely a reflection, of reading proficiency. (302)

However, The National Reading Panel rejected the findings of the 1988 study, on the grounds that it does not meet their scientific research standards. The good news is that in 2004, Dr. S. Jay Samuels and Dr. Yi-Chen Wu completed a scientific study in response to the National Reading Panel and concluded that the more time students read, the higher their achievement compared to a control group. Samuels' and Wu's scientific research corroborated the conclusions of Anderson, Wilson, and Fielding.

Nancie Atwell also links daily reading to developing proficiency in reading books every day (2014). Volume in reading is an effective intervention for developing readers (Allington 1977, 2011; Allington and Gabriel, 2012; Allington and McGill-Franzen 2021) and a predictor of learning success because students who read perform better on standardized tests in reading, vocabulary, and writing than do students who read little to no books (Krashen 2004).

TABLE 1.1. Variation in Amount of Independent Reading. From Anderson, Richard C., et al. "Growth in Reading and How Children Spend Their Time Outside of School." *Reading Research Quarterly*, vol. 23, no. 3, 1988, pp. 285–303.

Percentile Rank for Reading Volume	Minutes a Day	Words a Year
98th	67.3	4,733,000
90th	33.4	2,375,000
70th	16.9	1,168,000
50th	9.2	601,000
30th	4.3	251,000
10th	1.0	51,000
2nd	0.0	______

Richard Allington recommends that children read in all subjects throughout the school day to maintain volume in reading (2013). To reach this goal, schools can support volume in reading for students in seven ways:

1. Classroom Libraries. Bridget Wilson, a fifth-grade ELA inclusion teacher, describes the benefits of a classroom library: "Having a classroom library ensures our ability to check off many of the things we all consider essential for our students. As teachers, we can feel good knowing that a great classroom library can increase the quality of student discussion, encourage choice, inform, motivate, and excite students at any level. A varied and rich class library will provide our students opportunities for acceptance, inclusion, and informed citizenry. Having a vast and inclusive collection of books at our students' fingertips will not only help them check out stacks of books to read, but as their reading increases so will their skill and critical thinking."

As you develop your classroom library, it's important to have books by Black, Latinx, Asian Americans, Native Americans, Muslim Americans—in other words, books need to represent the cultural diversity of our country. Besides fiction and poetry, ELA and content teachers need to choose nonfiction books that show students the achievements of diverse cultures and include books about scientists, mathematicians, doctors, lawyers, scholars, political activists, dancers, musicians, artists, actors, journalists, and sports greats. White students and students of color need to understand that the contributions to our society and the world represent the diversity that defines our nation!

A solid classroom starter library has about 600 books. However, you should strive to have 1,000 to 1,500 books in your classroom library if you teach English. If you teach science, social studies, math, physical education, or the fine arts, aim for 200–250 books in classroom libraries. Books in content subjects move students beyond the limits of textbook learning and can increase their depth of knowledge of a topic. Sports teachers in several schools I've worked with have collaborated with English teachers to have a "sports and health section" in classroom libraries.

Invite students to spread the word about beloved books and reserve time in your class to present a sixty-second elevator talk and advertise to peers a book they enjoyed.

Sixty-Second Elevator Talk

Here are some tips for presenting a brief talk that captures listeners' interest.

Jot notes that:

- Recap an exciting part.
- Explain why the book's a great read.
- End with an intriguing question, a unique idea from the book, or an inspirational quote from the book.

Unfortunately, there are some schools where the media specialists and other staff believe classroom libraries compete with the school's media center. Not so. School media centers have much larger collections than classroom libraries and a specialist who knows all the books. In most schools, students visit the media center once a week to check out books, and this doesn't offer them the daily access to replace books they've completed that a classroom library does. You can avoid limiting students' access to books by having the media specialist work closely with teachers to form trusting relationships that result in supporting one another.

2. Independent Reading of Self-Selected Books. Often, because teachers leave independent reading as the last experience students have in English classes, it doesn't happen. However, if daily independent reading is the practice students need to develop their reading skill and stamina, then it's crucial that teachers in grades 5 through 12 intentionally set aside time at the start of class for students to self-select books and read. In October 2019, NCTE posted a position statement on independent reading that opens with:

> Independent reading leads to an increased reading volume of reading. The more one reads, the better one reads. The more one reads, the more knowledge of words and language one acquires. The more one reads, the more fluent one becomes as a reader. The more one reads, the easier it becomes to sustain the mental effort necessary to comprehend complex texts. The more one reads, the more one learns about the people and happenings of our world. This increased volume of reading is essential. (Allington 2014)

Daily independent reading also develops stamina, the ability of students to focus on reading as well as recall and understand what they've read for at least thirty minutes. Equally important, books offer students mirrors of their own life experiences and windows into the lives of others (Bishop 1990). As students choose books and read, they can experience life in the past, present, and future.

They also can develop an awareness of how others live and interact as well as explore topics that broaden their knowledge of the world beyond their school and community. When schools invest in classroom libraries in all subjects, they create access to books for students throughout the school day.

3. Instructional Reading. One novel or one grade-level program for all students diminishes students' reading volume because if a group of students can't read the materials, they're sliding backward, avoiding reading, and developing negative attitudes. You can organize instructional reading around a genre, a theme, a genre and a theme, or a core book and contemporary related books and have multiple texts for students so they read at their instructional reading levels (see chapters five and six).

4. Alternate Texts in Science and Social Studies. Now students read in ELA class and the media center, but as they move through other content subjects, reading stops for below grade-level readers because textbooks are too difficult. Volume in reading matters for all students, but it especially matters for learners who read below grade level. To help developing readers make progress, they need to read more than students reading at or above grade level (Allington 1977, 2007, 2011). That's why reading in one class a day is not enough volume to raise students' reading skills. In his article "Intervention All Day Long: New Hope for Struggling Readers" (2007), Richard Allington writes:

> We need to reconceptualize intervention for struggling readers as something that must occur all day long. Intervention cannot just consist of those few minutes working with a reading specialist. Let's face the fact that too often, the texts in students' hands are appropriate for the highest achieving half of students, ensuring that the rich get richer because only the best readers have books in their hands that they can read fluently, and with understanding. All students need texts of an appropriate level of complexity all day long to thrive in school. (13)

Moreover, students who can't complete the reading also can't participate in discussions and be productive members of collaborative learning. With the assistance of the media specialist, content teachers can order books on the topics they teach that developing readers can learn from. Now students can read in every class, and each day, volume increases their reading competency.

5. School Media Centers. Truly the heart and hub of a school, today's media centers are much more than a place to check out books. They tap into students' creative thinking and problem-solving abilities with makerspaces, comfortable spaces to read, and collaborative spaces where students can discuss books and plan projects. The media specialist can support research projects by finding materials for students that teachers can check out and bring to their classrooms. Besides book talks about new books with students, the media specialist often publishes a bimonthly list of new books for staff and highlights a few in book talks at faculty and department meetings.

In schools where classroom teachers and the media specialist are a team, teachers seek input on books that might interest specific students and suggestions for culturally relevant texts, popular authors, and series to include in classroom libraries. Being a team ensures you're working for the same goals: including books that represent the diverse populations in our country and increasing every student's volume in reading.

6. Readers' Notebooks. Students have notebooks for responding to their reading, to teacher read-alouds, and to videos, book trailers, and photographs (Crowder 2020). I recommend readers' notebooks remain at school stored in a plastic crate, cardboard box, or on a bookshelf that's labeled with the class section or period in which it meets. Before class officially starts, have three to four students quickly give out notebooks. At the end of class, the same students return notebooks to the appropriate place. Avoid sending notebooks home, as you'll find that many don't come back the next day, and that's frustrating. Moreover, some don't appear for several days. Instead, have students complete writing about reading homework on separate paper. After you read their work and provide feedback, have students paste each homework entry into their notebooks.

For writing about reading to encourage volume in reading, students need to share and discuss notebook entries. It's during the sharing and talking that students learn about books peers couldn't put down. In middle and high school, students value peer recommendations for reading far more than books adults promote. When eighth grader Ariel listened to Masha read her notebook entry on *The Fog of Forgetting* by G. A. Morgan, Ariel, a devotee of horse stories, checked out the book when Masha completed it. In a conference, Ariel told me that because Masha was so excited about the book and couldn't wait to start *The Kinfolk*, the next in the series, Ariel decided to give the fantasy novel a try.

You can also create a bulletin board for students to write on sticky notes the title and author of a book and one sentence explaining why they enjoyed reading it.

Vary how students exchange notebook entries about books by inviting them to share with different partners or in a small group. Then, periodically, reserve time for students to read these comments.

7. Daily Teacher Read-Alouds. By reserving time to read aloud every day, you have dozens of opportunities to share poems, short stories, short biographies, myths, folktales, articles, and excerpts from texts as well as introduce students to a variety of genres and authors. Read aloud short and long texts that represent the diversity in our country and introduce students to authors such as Nikki Grimes, Janet Wong, Gwendolyn Brooks, Nic Stone, Lamar Giles, Ibi Zoboi, Yusef Saalam, Elizabeth Acevedo, Julian Randall, Yesenia Montilla, Angie Thomas, Nicola Yoon, Sabaa Tahir, Jason Reynolds, as well as Marie Lu, Celia C. Pérez, Aisha Saeed, Joseph Bruchac, Samira Ahmed, Julia Alvarez, and Pablo Cartaya, to name a few. You'll also telegraph the message that these authors are important to you and that students will enjoy reading their books.

I recommend that you make the text available to students after you've completed it. Feature books on the chalkboard tray and on your desk or in a special place if it's a short text you downloaded from the internet. Recently, a seventh-grade teacher I was coaching read a few short stories from *Take the Mic: Fictional Stories of Everyday Resistance* (2019), and ten students wrote their names on the chalkboard under "Read-Alouds I Want to Read." Fortunately, the teacher was able to purchase two additional copies, making access easier.

If you have a short class period, choose a poem, a short article, or a short narrative to read aloud. You are also modeling fluent, expressive reading and selecting a text that encourages students to think and talk about a concept, specific topic, theme, genre, and the beauty of the language. Besides exploring texts for daily read-alouds, I invite you to set aside time to reflect on your own personal reading life.

Teachers Need a Personal Reading Life

Whether you're a scientist reading about climate change to narrow the focus of your hypothesis, a math teacher who knows students need to read well to be able to unpack word problems, or an English teacher having students read science fiction, reading to learn is an important part of your discipline. Yes, it's important to read and to know the literature that relates to the content you teach; that's a given. But it's also important for you to carve out time to develop your own reading life, for doing this enables you to talk to students about recent books you enjoyed. It also enlarges your understanding of the value of volume in reading: building vocabulary, improving recall and comprehension, and developing a clearer understanding of a specific text structure. The more you connect to yourself as a reader, the better you are able to make connections with and for students. For example, when sixth grader Oscar told me during a conference, "When I read on my own, I like graphic novels; I can stick with it and get into the story."

I was able to reply, "You know, I like to read magazines and mysteries on my own because even if I'm tired, I can read them. It's okay to read books that are pure fun."

Oscar looked befuddled at first, and then said, "Yeah. I'm. .. I'm reading. . ."

"That's what counts," I told him.

And Oscar grinned.

A personal reading life enables you to experience the power of visualizing as a path to understanding, the need to talk to someone about a book resonating with you, and that sometimes, reading can be challenging work. Your enthusiasm for and engagement in reading can rub off on students as they choose books they want to and can read, ensuring they will be engaged.

Nurturing and growing your personal reading life can familiarize you with culturally diverse books and poems to use for daily read-alouds as well as include these texts in your instructional reading units of study and classroom library.

Keeping in Touch with Your Reading Life

When Donald Graves spoke at national conferences, he often encouraged teachers to stay in touch with their own literacy so they could better understand how to support, build, and enhance students' literate lives. When you experience the need to focus deeply on reading and the pleasures of self-selection, discovering new authors, new topics, and returning to favorite genres, you recognize what good readers do and can share your personal experiences with students.

Closing Reflections: Collaborative Conversations

Meet with a colleague or your grade-level team or department and have conversations about ideas presented in this chapter that can challenge the status quo as well as nudge you to risk changing teaching and learning practices.

- Why is it important to tweak your class schedule so independent reading is front and center?
- Why does culturally relevant teaching affect the books you read aloud, use for instruction, and add to your classroom library? Why is this important for all students?

- Why is volume in reading the key to developing expertise for all readers but especially for developing readers?
- How can the seven pillars of engagement increase students' reading volume?

As You Continue to Read

Explore the next six chapters to see how you can increase students' volume in reading.

Chapter 2 looks at white privilege curricula, suggests how teachers can confront their personal biases, and provides tips for developing units that reflect the diversity in our country. You'll also explore ideas for integrating technology into your lessons.

Chapter 3 takes a deep dive into independent reading and how it enlarges specific reading skills and volume. You'll also explore and reflect on authentic assessments and guidelines for implementing each one.

Chapter 4 discusses ways to integrate small-group instruction into your English classes to provide brief but effective interventions, support, and reteaching for all students.

Chapter 5 discusses developing instructional reading libraries organized around a genre and related theme with books that represent the diverse reading needs of your students.

Chapter 6 shows how you can increase reading volume using core collections: a required core text and contemporary related texts. By gathering books related the core text's themes on diverse instructional reading levels, students can have choices and read far beyond the one required text.

Chapter 7 provides suggestions for ELA teachers for getting started and moving forward and the benefits of classroom libraries for math, social studies, and science teachers.

2 Teaching with Intentionality

May 25, 2020, forever changed the United States of America. On that day, Americans watched a video that showed George Floyd, a forty-six-year-old African American man, handcuffed, gasping for breath, and dying as a police officer knelt on his throat for seven minutes and forty-six seconds. George Floyd's death, watched by millions of Americans, ignited the Black Lives Matter movement and massive protests by culturally diverse groups from all over our country.

During the summer of 2020, calls to end systemic racism, mass incarceration of Black and Brown men, and inequities in education reverberated around the country. Though progressive changes in education come slowly, Black Lives Matter demonstrations revealed that it's time for educators and schools to confront Eurocentric, white-privileged curricula and develop culturally responsive and relevant curricula and teaching (Espana and Herrera 2020; Osario 2020). The collaborative process schools initiate will be ongoing as school leadership and staff read, study, and engage in reflective conversations that can raise awareness of needed changes and explore pathways to achieve them (DiAngelo 2018; Joseph 2020; Kay 2018; Kendi 2019).

Conversations among teachers and students can be difficult, as levels of discomfort frequently arise when confronting racism, white privilege, and feelings of entitlement. These issues have been part of our culture since the onset of the slave trade and slavery, and they can be seen today in the mass incarceration of Black and Brown men and the treatment of immigrant populations. Moreover, such beliefs and traditions have divided our country into two groups: the group that has power (oppressors) and the groups that are powerless (oppressed).

In 1968, Paolo Friere published *Pedagogy of the Oppressed*. His thoughts about oppression are relevant today and support the agenda of Black Lives Matter and antiracism thinking. Freire explains that a goal of the oppressed is to identify their oppressors and through dialogue recognize that the goals of oppressors are materialistic—wealth, power, and control—and then win back their humanity and place in society through education and further dialogue. In the preface to the original English edition published in 1970, Richard Schaull explains that according to Friere:

> Education either functions as an instrument which is used to facilitate integration of the younger generation into the logic of the present system and bring about conformity or it becomes the practice of freedom, the means by which men and women deal critically and creatively with reality and discover how to participate in the transformation of the world. (219)

These words, ". . . or becomes the practice of freedom by which men and women deal critically and creatively with reality and discover how to participate in the transformation of the world," provide a path for educators to bring about access, equity, justice, and equal opportunity to all groups. To "participate in the transformation of the world," school leaders and teachers have to discover where they are with white privilege and racism. This first step to disrupting the status quo in education should be followed by creating a curriculum that offers students diverse texts and materials—a curriculum that represents our nation's cultural diversity (DiAngelo 2018; Kay 2018; Kendi 2019; Muhammad 2020). Freire believes that teachers and the texts they use with students can shape learners' views of history, making it imperative for educators to offer students historically accurate texts and to develop students' critical and creative thinking. In addition, teachers need to sharpen students' ability to recognize bad policies, lies, and conspiracy theories on social media and in newspapers, so they can use this skill to become the informed citizens our democracy needs.

Kendi makes the point that bad policies, not bad people, cause racial inequities, and like Freire, he encourages people to identify the groups that perpetuate inequities and work for change (Freire 1968; Kendi 2019). To root out and remove oppressive policies and traditions in education and replace them with access, equity, justice, and equal opportunity requires intentional decisions from school leaders and teachers. Being intentional can lead them to face the pressing need for disrupting and changing thinking based on inaccurate history and then to consciously explore ways to accomplish transformations (DiAngelo 2018; Freire 1968. 2018; Kendi 2019; Kay 2018). So we're all on the same page, I've included definitions of key terms used in this chapter, and I've used Kendi's definitions for the first three terms.

Racist: A person who, through their actions, words, or inactions, supports and expresses racist ideas, such as one racial group has superior intelligence compared to other groups.

Antiracist: A person who, through their actions and words, expresses antiracist ideas and supports antiracist policies and strives to create equity among all groups.

Racial Inequities: When two or more racial groups aren't on equal footing. Examples are racial inequality in education, housing, healthcare, and job opportunities.

Structural Racism refers to systems that maintain and control the inequities of racism and white privilege. It can be seen in housing, educational and job opportunities, access to medical care, the justice system, wages, and purchasing power that accepts white leadership and power over Americans from different cultural backgrounds.

Systemic Racism is a form of racism embedded in a society and accepted as the norm by those in power. It's evident in mass incarceration of Black and brown men and stark inequities in education, healthcare, employment and wages, and political power.

White Privilege is the acceptance of white superiority as the norm and reveals itself in the inherent advantages given to white people—books and learning materials, skilled teachers, educational opportunities, job opportunities, housing, leadership roles, and acquisition of wealth.

Access and Equity: Access in education means the system is fair and inclusive and all the advantages—books and materials, labs, libraries, skilled teachers, a well-equipped building, etc.—found in high-performing suburban schools are available to all schools. Equity means that educational policies and teaching methods respond to students' individual needs, resulting in all students having equal opportunities.

The Deficit Model often erodes students' self-confidence and increases their frustration because the expectations are that underserved students can do better and achieve if they'd only work harder, listen carefully, and complete the assigned work.

Be Intentional about Changing Bad Policies

Making a commitment to examine your school's curriculum and your personal beliefs regarding access, equity, justice, and opportunity rests with the principal of your school. By encouraging conversations and helping teachers feel safe as they honestly explore and confront their biases and share feelings about the school's curriculum, the principal creates an environment that can result in positive changes.

This is not a one-and-done meeting. It will require ongoing scheduled opportunities where groups share thoughts and reflect on some of the terms above to assess where they are and how to change their thinking. Moreover, a series of conversations should occur each year for the benefit of new staff and also address and revisit practices and beliefs such as the deficit model, the "low" students, the achievement gap, grading policies, poverty and its effects on learning, and punishments for unacceptable behavior and incomplete work. Because our personal experiences with education have created a set of racist beliefs accepted for generations, the process of change will be accompanied with discomfort and at times anger and defensive words and actions (Kay 2018; Kendi 2019; Minor 2018). Expecting these feelings can make it easier to deal with taking a long look at your beliefs and teaching.

Some traditional educational beliefs such as deficit models and "low" achievers can reduce students' opportunities at school and in the workforce. If you're in the "low" group and are always receiving low grades and expected to learn from materials you can't read and comprehend and aren't relevant to your life and heritage, then your future in and out of school can differ from students who have white privilege, strong literacy skills, and parents who can help them with schoolwork or have the financial means to hire a tutor.

The ancient Taoist philosopher Lao Tzu wrote: "If you correct your mind, the rest of your life will fall into place." Questions can shine a spotlight on inequities and the need to "correct" our thinking. It's the learning, reflection, and conversations that can lead us to adjust and refine how we think about teaching, curriculum, and white privilege.

Getting Started

Candid discussions about white privilege, racism, and deficit models can be introduced by the superintendent of a district, by the principal, and by teachers. Positive changes are more likely to occur in a school where the principal and other administrators continually build trusting relationships among staff, encourage teacher leadership and feedback, and set aside time to have ongoing conversations with individuals and small groups.

When the principal opens the first meeting stating something like: *We're here to examine some school practices that we can and must change. Even if it makes us feel uncomfortable, we all have racist thoughts and can make racist statements—the point is to be able to recognize when this occurs and use this knowledge to change. In our school, I want us to look at the one-size-fits-all novels in ELA classes, texts used in history classes, and the deficit model that often creeps into my thinking when we discuss our Black and Lantinx students,* then teachers will feel more comfortable in honestly assessing where they are. As the principal creates an environment in which staff members feel they can risk reflecting on where they stand with these issues, they then can begin to grapple with bad policies.

Since discussions about white privilege, racism, and deficit models increase participants' anxiety and discomfort, it's best to meet with small groups rather than the entire faculty. Meeting with grade-level teams or specific departments creates a safer environment for sharing because members know one another well. It's helpful if the principal or assistant principal facilitate each group's first meeting and then attend subsequent meetings by rotating among groups. Ask group members to bring a journal, so they can keep a record of their questions, conversations, and monitor their philosophical changes and actions taken to adjust and refine curriculum and texts available to students (Singleton 2021).

After the first meeting, consider opening the next meeting with the principal or assistant principal posing a guiding question, such as: *How can we become culturally responsive and relevant teachers, and where are we with this kind of teaching?* (See pages 21–22 for an explanation of culturally responsive and relevant teaching.) Allowing quiet time for reflection and writing in notebooks and then discussing the guiding question can generate additional questions for pairs or small groups to discuss, write about, and share. Below is a compilation of some questions teachers raised in different schools.

- Which students does our present curriculum reach?
- What makes materials culturally relevant?
- Our school population is 95 percent white. Why do we need to have culturally relevant materials?
- How do we meet the diverse needs of our student population?
- What's wrong with the deficit model?
- Why are white-privileged texts racist?
- Why do we doubt an excellent score on a test or the well-written essays of Black or Brown students?
- Will students stop working if we don't give lots of grades?
- What are some "bad policies" in our schools? How can we change these?
- What kinds of changes do we need to make to become culturally responsive and relevant teachers?
- How does structural racism affect our staff, students, and families?
- How can we keep a positive white identity based on equity instead of feelings of superiority?
- What work must we do to change racism in our school?
- Why is it important to learn the truth about the racist history of our country?
- How can we develop a positive antiracist white identity in ourselves and in the students we teach?

Once teachers express an interest in reading and discussing books relating to their inquiry, they can investigate books listed on this page and/or suggest additional books of their own.

Moving toward Culturally Responsive and Relevant Teaching

Moving toward culturally responsive and relevant teaching requires time to study, introspection, and self-evaluation to think about and learn where you are with racism, antiracism, white privilege, deficit models, and grading. As you continue to work on rethinking bad policies, start reviewing how you're using books in your classroom.

Adding inclusive books to your classroom library is a first step, but it's not enough. Not every student will choose to read an inclusive text, nor will they see these as important to their learning unless culturally relevant texts become part of your read-alouds, instructional units, book clubs, and literature circles. During NCTE's 2020 Virtual Convention, authors Lamar Giles, Nic Stone, and Ibi Zoboi explained that it was tough growing up and reading books with characters they didn't relate to and how important it is for all students to see themselves in books and in their communities. In 1990, Dr. Rudine Sims Bishop published an essay about providing students with diverse books that reflect "the multicultural nature of the world."

During NCTE's 2020 virtual Convention, author Bettina Love stated, "Education can't save us; we have to save education." By reading professional books and literature by authors who have experienced systemic and structural racism, teachers and school leaders can lean into their discomfort and begin working on transforming bad educational policies into equitable policies for everyone.

Professional Books

Cultivating Genius: An Equity Framework for Culturally and Historically Responsive Literacy by Gholdy Muhammad

How to Be an Antiracist by Ibram X. Kendi

Not Light, but Fire: How to Lead Meaningful Race Conversations in the Classroom by Matthew R. Kay

The Black Friend: On Being a Better White Person by Frederick Joseph

We Got This.: Equity, Access, and the Quest to Be Who Our Students Need Us to Be by Cornelius Minor

White Fragility: Why It's So Hard for White People to Talk about Racism by Robin DiAngelo

Contemporary Literature

All American Boys by Jason Reynolds and Brendan Kiely

Dear Martin by Nic Stone

Internment by Samira Ahmed

Punching the Air by Ibi Zoboi and Yusef Salaam

Stamped: Racism, Antiracism, and You by Jason Reynolds and Ibram X. Kendi

The Hate U Give by Angie Thomas

They Called Us Enemy by George Takei

> Books are sometimes windows, offering views of worlds that may be real or imagined, familiar or strange. These windows are also sliding glass doors, and readers have only to walk through in imagination to become part of whatever world has been created and recreated by the author. When lighting conditions are just right, however, a window can also be a mirror. Literature transforms human experience and reflects it back to us, and in that reflection we can see our own lives and experiences as part of the larger human experience. Reading, then, becomes a means of self-affirmation, and readers often seek their mirrors in books. (ix–xi)

Whether your classes are all white or represent the cultural diversity of our country and the world, your students deserve to see themselves in books. Learners can better understand who they are by reading about characters like them, but they also need to use their imaginations to step into the skins of characters different from them and see the world through their eyes. "Mirrors, windows, and sliding glass doors"—this type of reading offers countless opportunities to empathize with characters whose lives differ from ours as well as to understand their struggles, hopes, dreams, anger, and frustrations. I recall a white high school student telling me how unprepared he felt when participating in a mock United Nations in Chicago; he was angry that his education up to that point was one of white privilege. Bad policies such as a white-privileged curriculum in an all-white school do our students a disservice because they're unprepared to positively interact with people whose lives differ from theirs.

One of George Santayana's famous aphorisms is "Those who cannot remember the past are condemned to repeat it." The problem we face today, in addition to not remembering our history. is that many are unaware of the history of the slave trade, slavery, and Jim Crow laws that still exist and persist today. A good start is having middle and high school students read *Stamped: Racism, Antiracism, and You* by Jason Reynolds and Ibram X. Kendi (2020). Their book examines America's racist past and present by showing how and when racist ideas started and spread. Then, the authors proceed to discredit each historical misrepresentation by shining lights on the truth.

Santayana's words also include knowing and remembering the past by reading historical fiction that provides accurate portrayals of characters as they lived their lives in diverse historical eras. You can elevate Bishop's calls for "mirrors, windows, and sliding glass doors" by integrating inclusive and culturally relevant texts into your curriculum.

Bring Culturally Relevant Texts into Your Curriculum

Bring sustainable changes to your curriculum by integrating culturally relevant texts into your daily lessons in meaningful ways. For me, meaningful ways invites you to feature culturally diverse voices so students come to value, understand, and respect the lives and problems of those they don't know. No matter the demographics of your school and community, offer culturally relevant books so no group feels marginalized (Germán 2021; Vaughn and Massey 2021).

Teacher read-alouds should include a variety of genres that reflect the cultural diversity in the world. Reading aloud historically accurate novels like Nic Stone's *Clean Getaway* (2020) and picture books such as *The First Step: How One Girl Put Segregations on Trial* by Susan E. Goodman, illustrated by E. B. Lewis (2016), reveal how much you value the story of "us" and not of only one group.

Reading units can provide a more historically accurate view of the world's past, present, and future when students read and discuss books that represent the world—books where they see themselves and books where they learn about other cultures and traditions. In chapter five, I explain how to organize diverse instructional libraries, and in chapter six, you'll explore how high school English teachers can teach a core required book such as *The Scarlet Letter* and find a wide range of inclusive contemporary books related to one or more themes in the core book.

Text sets invite you to organize books around a theme, such as friendship, or a topic, such as segregation, that includes a variety of genres and reading levels so all members of a text set group can read, learn, collaborate, and contribute to conversations. Text sets that have different genres offer readers opportunities to see a theme or topic from diverse perspectives. Your school's media specialist and/or your local public librarian can help you develop text sets for groups to read and discuss. On page 24 you'll find two examples of text sets: one for middle school and one for high school.

When you develop culturally responsive and relevant units of study, you begin to help students eradicate the "us' versus "them" outlook; you debunk the political myths of oppression and move toward more equitable and culturally relevant teaching (Germán 2021). All of us need time to reflect on and face the historical truths that diverse texts present—texts such as books, essays, poems, podcasts, movies, photographs, and videos, etc. An excellent strategy to start students on this journey is to invite them to read and discuss texts that are historically accurate and inspirational.

Middle School Text Sets on Friendship

Bronx Masquerade by Nikki Grimes (poetry and personal essays)

Clean Getaway by Nic Stone (fiction)

The Friendship by Mildred Taylor (fiction)

Each Kindness by Jacqueline Woodson (picture book, fiction)

Enchanted Air: Two Cultures, Two Wings by Margarita Engle (memoir)

Love to Langston by Tony Medina (poems)

The Maze Runner: Book 1 by Jams Dashner (science fiction)

Two Roads by Joseph Bruchac (fiction)

They Call Us Enemy by George Takei (graphic novel)

High School Text Sets on Segregation

Green Book (DVD, movie)

Freedom: A Photographic History of the African American Struggle by Manning Marable and Leith Mullings (photographs)

How Fascism Works: The Politics of Us and Them by Jason Stanley (nonfiction)

The Hate U Give by Angie Thomas (fiction)

I Am Not Your Perfect Mexican Daughter by Erika L. Sánchez (fiction)

Turning 15 on the Road to Freedom by Lynda Blackmon Lowery (memoir)

March: Book One by John Lewis, Andrew Aydin, and Nate Powell (graphic memoir)

The Poet Slave of Cuba: A Biography of Juan Francisco Manzano by Margarita Engle, illustrated by Sean Qualls (poetry)

The Absolutely True Diary of a Part-Time Indian by Sherman Alexie (fiction)

Evaluating and Choosing Books for Instruction and Classroom Libraries

If you're fortunate enough to have a media specialist and/or a relationship with your area's public librarian, ask them to recommend and help you evaluate books to be added to your classroom library and those you plan to use for instruction. You can also read online reviews and recommendations in *School Library Journal*, *Language Arts*, and *The Horn Book*, as well as explore websites listed on page 25.

To help you create a diverse book collection for independent and instructional reading and for daily read-alouds, reflect on these seven questions:

- Do the books include main and minor LGBTQAI+ characters, disabled characters, characters of color, as well as characters that represent the culturally diversity in our country and the world?

- Are the books historically and culturally accurate?
- Do the books' authors and illustrators represent diverse cultures and lifestyles?
- Does your collection include picture books, poetry, fiction, nonfiction, essays, and drama?
- Do the books serve as "mirrors, windows, and sliding glass doors" for all students in your classes?
- Will the books lead students to depth of thinking and hold the possibilities of changing their beliefs or increasing their empathy and understanding?
- Do books already in your collections contain racial, ethnic, and societal stereotypes in the text and/or images? How do you plan to counter these stereotypes?

Websites to Explore for Culturally Relevant Books

Multicultural Children's Book Day
https://multiculturalchildrensbookday.com

Multicultural and Social Justice Books
https://socialjusticebooks.org

ALA Youth Media Awards
http://www.ala.org/awardsgrants/awards/browse/yma?showfilter=no

Diversity in YA
https://diversityinya.tumblr.com

Where Can I Find Great Diverse Children's Books?
https://blog.leeandlow.com/2014/03/21/where-can-i-find-great-diverse-childrens-books/

Colours of Us—All About Multicultural Children's Books
https://coloursofus.com

Nerdy Book Club
https://nerdybookclub.wordpress.com

The choices you offer students and the books you select to read aloud have the power to invade students' hearts and minds by raising emotions, generating questions, and inviting them to think deeply about stories, poems, informational texts, and plays.

Books to Start Students' Conversations about White Privilege and Racism

As a white teacher I find that, for me, the best way to start students thinking about racism and white privilege is by inviting them to read and discuss books that can raise their awareness of issues such as mass incarceration, unequal opportunities, structural and systemic racism, and white privilege (Kay 2018; Singleton 2021). You can also use current events articles about Black Lives Matter and the insurrection at our nation's capitol on January 6, 2021.

Before organizing student conversations about diverse texts, offer them choices and provide them with information about texts they can select through book talks you present or by setting aside time for students to browse through texts. Students can start by generating questions a text raises and then share their emotional reactions and suggestions for change through conversations.

Whole class discussions can be an excellent starting point. I recommend using short texts such as poems, photographs, short stories, or videos so you and your students can discuss a text in one class. Students require time, and discussions might spill over to the next time class meets. Summarize the key points students made at the end of class and review these the next day prior to continuing conversations.

Partner conversations work well, whether pairs select the same text or discuss two different texts and share their questions, feelings, and what they've learned.

Literature circles invite small groups of students to read and discuss the same text. Students can select a common text from several you offer or they can suggest a movie on DVD, a video, photographs, or paintings that they can study, reflect upon, and discuss.

It's impossible to monitor all partner and small-group discussions. I find I learn more by listening to one discussion and gaining insights into other discussions by inviting students to develop a bulleted list in their notebooks of:

- big ideas discussed,
- questions members raised,
- opposing perspectives or ideas,
- events and/or information that changed their thinking,
- issues and events that roused strong emotions, and
- suggestions for initiating change.

Know that discussions of racism, white privilege, and/or the criminal justice system require time for students to think, raise questions, process, and share. Ten to fifteen minutes won't cut it—think in terms of entire class periods (Kay 2018; Robb 2017).

Be prepared for students' conversations to include anger, frustration, denial, and racist comments. Listen carefully. Let students be in charge of the conversation unless you feel it's necessary to redirect a heated discussion. You can help students change direction with a question, a statement for them to react to, by stating what you're noticing

Learn More about Student-Led Conversations

If you're unsure about preparing students to lead literary conversations, you can explore these books:

Not Light, but Fire by Matthew R. Kay

Read, Talk, Write by Laura Robb

and inviting them to use text examples to support their ideas, or by stopping the discussion and allowing them to cool off before continuing the discussion during the next class.

Discussions can occur in class, but they can also occur online, if your school uses virtual learning. Now that students have experienced online conversations during COVID-19, it's possible to invite students to initiate new conversations with a partner or a small group about texts and issues as a homework assignment.

Virtual/Hybrid Learning and Student Book Discussions

Before initiating online student conversations about books, you'll need to build trusting relationships with students to begin to know one another. The suggestions that follow work in virtual and in-class learning and should continue throughout the school year.

Share your stories. Talk about what you did on holidays and during the summer, especially what you enjoy doing in your free time. Share books, movies, series, and other texts you're enjoying. Help students know you as a person, so they can relate to you and see that both groups share common experiences.

Meet one-on-one with students to learn about their outside-of-school life. Keep visits short—about three to five minutes—but repeat them, for it's in the repetition that relationships start. Here are some questions you might pose to start the conversation:

- What do you enjoy doing at home in your free time?
- Do you have a favorite sport that you watch? That you play? Would you like to learn? Why do you enjoy watching and/or participating?
- Do you have brothers and/or sisters? What do you enjoy doing together?
- When do you see friends after school? What do you and your friends do together?
- Do you have any hobbies? What are they, and why do you enjoy them?

Once you know individuals, organize them into groups of two to four—groups you feel will be at ease talking and listening to one another.

Meet with small groups for five to ten minutes at first. You can extend the time as students reveal that they're enjoying building relationships. Once groups meet two to four times, you can reorganize them so everyone has opportunities to converse. Start by asking a question such as, *How did your evening go?*

or *What's on your mind?* You can also encourage students to volunteer and pose questions to spark discussion.

Students talking on their own offers opportunities for pairs and groups of three to four to have multiple opportunities to meet with different peers and strengthen relationships. This requires trust on your part and can start during school hours and continue after school and on weekends. Not only are you supporting and encouraging the development of trusting relationships, but you're also providing all students with ways to cultivate friendships.

Get to know students as readers once you've initiated building relationships with them and provided opportunities for students to get to know one another. Make sure you give students time to respond. Know that some students' answers will be negative. Be positive and praise students' honesty. I find it helpful to keep a log of my conferences with students about reading in an online journal or in a conference notebook. (Do the writing after the conference.) Here are some questions you can ask:

- How do you feel about reading? Explain why.
- Can you name a book you enjoyed listening to and explain why?
- Do you choose to read at home? What are you presently reading?
- Why do you think reading is important to you and your dreams?
- Do you have your own books? Can you name a few?
- Do other family members read? What kinds of texts do they read?
- Do you visit the public library in your community? How often? What kinds of books do you check out?
- Is there a book you read that changed how you think about people, life, friendships, war? Can you explain why the book changed you?
- Have you abandoned a book, or is there a book you wish you could have abandoned? Can you explain?

Make Reading Relevant to Students' Lives

Choices not only increase students' motivation and engagement, but choices bring relevance to each student's learning. Independent reading of self-selected books each time your class meets provides them with reading practice and also develops their literary tastes as they try different genres, topics, series, and authors. When instructional reading offers students choices, students select books they can read and learn from and become more invested in the reading (see chapters five and six). If you have flexibility in your curriculum and have four to five weeks for students to choose and direct their learning with your guidance and feedback, then consider inviting students to explore topics, theme, and authors.

For example, if a student wants to become an expert on the criminal justice system, explore a famous shipwreck, complete an author study of James Baldwin or Ernest Hemingway, or investigate the stereotyping of a specific group, they can work independently or with a partner. Their passion and interest can lead them to read fiction, nonfiction, poetry, and essays, watch movies and videos, visit museums through virtual tours of exhibits, conduct interviews and research, compile extensive notes, and then decide how they will present what they've learned to peers.

To help students develop plans that include texts and to monitor their work, have them submit the following: title of project; possible materials they plan to read and view (these can change as they complete the study); possible interviews. For each item, students can provide an estimated date of completion and a weekly or bimonthly date they will check in with you to ask questions, share notes, discuss what they've learned, and think about how they can share their project. Have one-on-one virtual meetings with students to monitor their progress and offer suggestions. If this is the first time you're inviting students to investigate topics they're passionate about, consider offering it to one section of students at a time to prevent feeling overwhelmed. Technology will not only enhance and increase their learning possibilities, but it will also enable them to keep detailed records of texts they've read and viewed as well as notes from research, interviews, and discussions.

Use Technology to Enhance Students' Learning

The goals of technology should be to enhance students' learning, deepen their understanding of specific content, and differentiate students' learning experiences, so they can be successful, participate and contribute, and move forward (Robb 2008; Tomlinson 2017). Schools use different technology platforms, and that's why it's best to work with your school's tech person to decide on the technology that best aligns with the teaching and learning technique you plan to use. You can view YouTube videos to deepen your knowledge of each one of the teaching techniques that follows as well as use a search engine to find professional articles and books.

Personalized learning is an approach that asks you to customize learning by considering each student's strengths, needs, and interests and use formative assessments to adjust their plan. You can place all students on individual learning plans for part of or for an entire unit or you can target students who require extra practice and then personalize their learning so they can master specific strategies (France 2019; Bray and McClaskey 2016). Technology enables you to offer students' choices in materials and how they can demonstrate their knowledge, understanding, and ability to think with specific content.

Blended learning, also called hybrid learning, asks teachers to integrate technology and digital media into classroom learning experiences and individualized students' learning (Tucker et al. 2016; Tucker 2018; Novak and Tucker 2021). Video plays an important role in delivering content to students and can be teacher-made videos or slides, digital learning stations, and YouTube videos on topics such as digital storytelling, digital assessment, and organizing digital portfolios.

Station learning can free you to support students who require reteaching of a lesson, an intervention that includes review and extra practice, or enrichment for students who already understand the lesson. Technology can help you set up stations for individuals, pairs, or small groups of students, who can work independently. This can include watching a video, analyzing photographs, or viewing a museum display related to their present studies, and then reading, discussing, and writing about the material (Lee 2019). The point is to use stations to differentiate the type of learning experiences you offer students as you move through a unit and respond to their needs based on formative and summative assessments (Tucker 2020). Supporting students throughout a unit of study can prevent small confusions from turning into challenges that require more time than you might have available.

Flipped learning relies heavily on technology, and students need access to a computer or tablet and the internet at home where they can view the teacher's lesson, demonstration, and/or read the assigned material. Teachers can then use class time for active learning, such as small-group work and providing individual attention for those needing support. In addition, during class, students can ask questions, collaborate to solve problems, and have discussions that provoke thinking and critical analysis (Carbaugh and Doubet 2015).

For schools to have an abundance of culturally relevant books, a culture of reading, and the technology to enhance how students learn, they need a principal who uses intentionality to spotlight the importance of culturally responsive and relevant teaching and how student engagement can lead to volume in reading.

Become a Reading Principal

By Evan Robb

As an adult, my personal and professional reading lives have sustained my desire to continually learn and read for pleasure. I value the fact that I can choose what to read, reread passages that speak to me, and talk about books and articles with friends and colleagues. These are values I hope to pass on to students and staff through two schoolwide initiatives.

To foster reading and bring culturally relevant texts and teaching to your school requires that you consider both initiatives: first, creating a culture of reading inclusive texts and then developing culturally responsive and relevant teaching in all subjects. Once each one has taken root, it's important to revisit them annually to discuss, adjust, and refine ideas as well as to develop new staff's understanding of each one. Leading both initiatives is the principal who models how much they value reading by supplying funds to enlarge and update classroom libraries and instructional reading units and by creating an inviting school media center with comfortable spaces for students to read. As a leader, you can impact both initiatives by collaborating with staff to create a yearlong meeting schedule with teams and/or departments.

Join Me! Let's create a culture of reading that represents our nation's diversity. Be the school leader who works with staff to collectively establish a school with:

- classroom libraries stocked with the finest books that represent our nation's diversity;
- a media center stocked with an exceptional collection of inclusive books, videos, and magazines;
- teachers who provide culturally diverse book choices for independent and instructional reading and daily read-alouds;
- a staff that celebrates reading by volunteering to read aloud to students; and
- students who always carry a book, eager to read at school and at home.

Initiate Conversations about Culturally Relevant Teaching and Books

As you collaborate with teachers to develop an inclusive culture of reading, it's also important to examine the books in classroom libraries, units of study, and your media center. The ideal cultural mix of books in libraries should include 50 percent by diverse authors, as this permits students to see themselves in books and to step into the skin of others to understand their lives. As you, other school leaders, and teachers examine books and materials and suggest recommendations, invite teachers to learn about culturally responsive and relevant teaching.

Having the books and materials is a first step, but how teachers integrate them into their lessons is equally important (Kay 2018; Muhammad 2020). Your first four to five meetings will have teams or departments discuss books and materials, create wish lists, and deepen their knowledge of culturally responsive and relevant teaching. These discussions will continue throughout the year and be revisited annually to continue the learning for everyone, to bring new hires up to speed, and to discuss any challenges that may arise. (See pages 21–26 for additional guidelines.) As you and groups of teachers converse, set aside time to consider what you can do, so students, staff, families, and the community think of your school as a place that values and promotes reading and then seek additional ideas from staff.

The Principal's Role in Creating a Culture of Reading

Short chunks of time with intentionality can advance a culture of reading in your school. Consider doing each of my five suggestions at least once a week.

- Visit classes and catch students reading—then positively reinforce what you see.
- Read aloud to a class.
- Post books you're reading during the year on your office door and invite teachers to do the same.
- Communicate to staff through your words, emails, and/or articles your commitment to independent reading and explain why.
- Send video messages to families about the importance of independent reading.

Commitments to both initiatives will send a positive message to students, staff, and families about your belief in reading and culturally responsive and relevant teaching. While this is happening, think ahead and consider the following questions to discuss with staff. I urge you to tape these questions to your desk, so you see them and reflect on them frequently to ensure you've communicated your vision for independent reading as well as engaged teachers in meaningful discussions to assess their needs and where they are with independent reading.

- Is independent reading a priority at my school? Are teachers reserving time for students to choose and read books during class?
- Do students keep an independent reading book on their desks, so they can read when they complete classwork?
- How can I encourage content teachers to develop subject-specific class libraries?
- Have I helped teachers understand that students don't need to write a summary, essay, or complete a project on each book?

Make It Happen!

Be intentional! Champion the reading of culturally diverse books and materials to develop a school full of readers. Remember, the room for improvement is the biggest room in every school. Enjoy the journey of creating culturally responsive and relevant teachers and a culture of reading that develops students' personal reading lives. Become the "reading principal" for your school!

Closing Reflections: Collaborative Conversations

Discuss these questions with a colleague or at a team or department meeting.

- Why is it important to have classroom libraries, media centers, and instructional units that include books and materials representing our country's diversity?
- How can you build relationships with and among students that support virtual learning?
- How can culturally responsive and relevant teaching increase equity and opportunity for students?
- How can technology enable you to differentiate instruction and intervention?

3 The Importance of Independent Reading

"You'll never make me read," an angry eighth grader tells me as she scans the bookcases in my classroom. It's early November, and her parents have recently moved to Winchester, Virginia. They tell me Katya is their third child, and her older brother and sister are both high achievers; both enjoy reading books at school and home—but not Katya. Teachers in her previous school all agree that Katya can decode—that is, say the words—and comprehend, but she only reads what's required.

I'm meeting Katya for the first time—before the school day officially begins. Inwardly, I tell myself that my goal will be to transform her into a reader. However, I reply, "Welcome to our class. And yes, you're right; I can't make you read."

"What's with the books—?"

But she doesn't complete her thought because students file into class and each retrieve a book from a shelf marked "Reserved" or take out a book they've been reading at home. A small disagreement over who will sit on the three oversized pillows today catches Katya's attention. I say nothing, knowing that these eighth graders can quickly resolve the issue by checking the "pillow rotation list." Soon, everyone has found a comfortable spot and is reading.

I show Katya to her desk, give her a reader's notebook, and explain that our class always opens with independent reading of self-selected books. Then, I invite her to browse through the books. She nods, walks over to the bookshelf stacked with magazines, chooses three, sits at her desk, and flips through pages. I say nothing, knowing that choosing a book and reading has to be her decision, and this will come once she finds a book that interests her—a book she can read and enjoy.

At the end of each month, students choose a book from a title and author log they keep and present a two-to-three minute book talk. Working from guidelines students created that invite thinking, analyzing, and reflecting, they prepare their thoughts on an index card and over two days present their book talks. Katya asks me, "Can I talk about a magazine?"

"Sure," I say. On book talk days, students can turn in a piece of scrap paper listing a book they'd like to read based on a peer's presentation. When Andrea book talks *Inside Out and Back Again* by Thanhha Lai, saying that she related to the book because her uncle fled Vietnam, I notice Katya staring at her. Andrea closes by stating that the book was in verse and that made it easier for her to read a longer book. At the end of class, Katya drops a reserve-this-book slip into the plastic tray on my desk and quickly exits the classroom.

Soon after Katya finishes *Inside Out and Back Again*, she tells me, "My parents fled Russia before I was born." Perhaps that was the connection to Lai's book—I don't ask. *She's reading*, I think, and that's all that matters. Katya is on a free-verse novel jag; she reads *Witness* and *Out of the Dust* by Karen Hesse, *Love That Dog* by Sharon Creech, but her favorite is *Bronx Masquerade* by Nikki Grimes.

Patience and time can change the reading attitudes of students who can read but, for reasons they can't or won't express, don't read. Patience and time are two gifts teachers can give, trusting that students will come to the reading life in a class that values their library and reading self-selected books. It's independent reading that can increase volume for students, and while they're immersed in a book they love, they are improving their reading skill and stamina.

Seven Foundational Skills That Independent Reading Supports

In the first chapter, I discussed how independent reading develops stamina, the ability to sustain the effort it takes to read for thirty minutes or longer. I also pointed out the research of Samuels and Wu, who concluded that volume in reading enlarges students' reading proficiency (2004). Reading proficiency includes the seven foundational skills that follow, for the seven work together to continually improve students' comprehension and critical and analytical thinking, as well as to develop empathy and compassion for others (NCTE 2019).

Background knowledge. The experiences and information students have about a topic, genre, or concept can support their recall and comprehension as well as their ability to analyze details in a text. By reading about the past, present, and future, by watching short videos on a topic, and by listening to you read aloud, students gain a wealth of background knowledge that can increase their comprehension and enjoyment of a text.

Fifth grader Shane Kim has been in America for two years. In a self-evaluation of her reading and understanding (figure 3.1), Shane draws pictures to show comprehension of vocabulary in the poem "Lost and Found" by David

Harrison (Robb and Harrison 2021). The poem, about Ryan Speedo Green, refers to opera and singing in an opera. Shane begins to understand opera after watching videos of Ryan Speedo Green singing and discussing his life. Without this background knowledge, Shane's comprehension of the poem would have been greatly diminished.

Vocabulary. Words are an important part of background knowledge, and if students don't have enough words for a topic, comprehension and recall can diminish. For example, a seventh-grade ELA teacher asks students to complete an "ABC List" prior to a unit on slavery and civil rights. In their notebooks, students write the letters of the alphabet on a page and next to each letter write

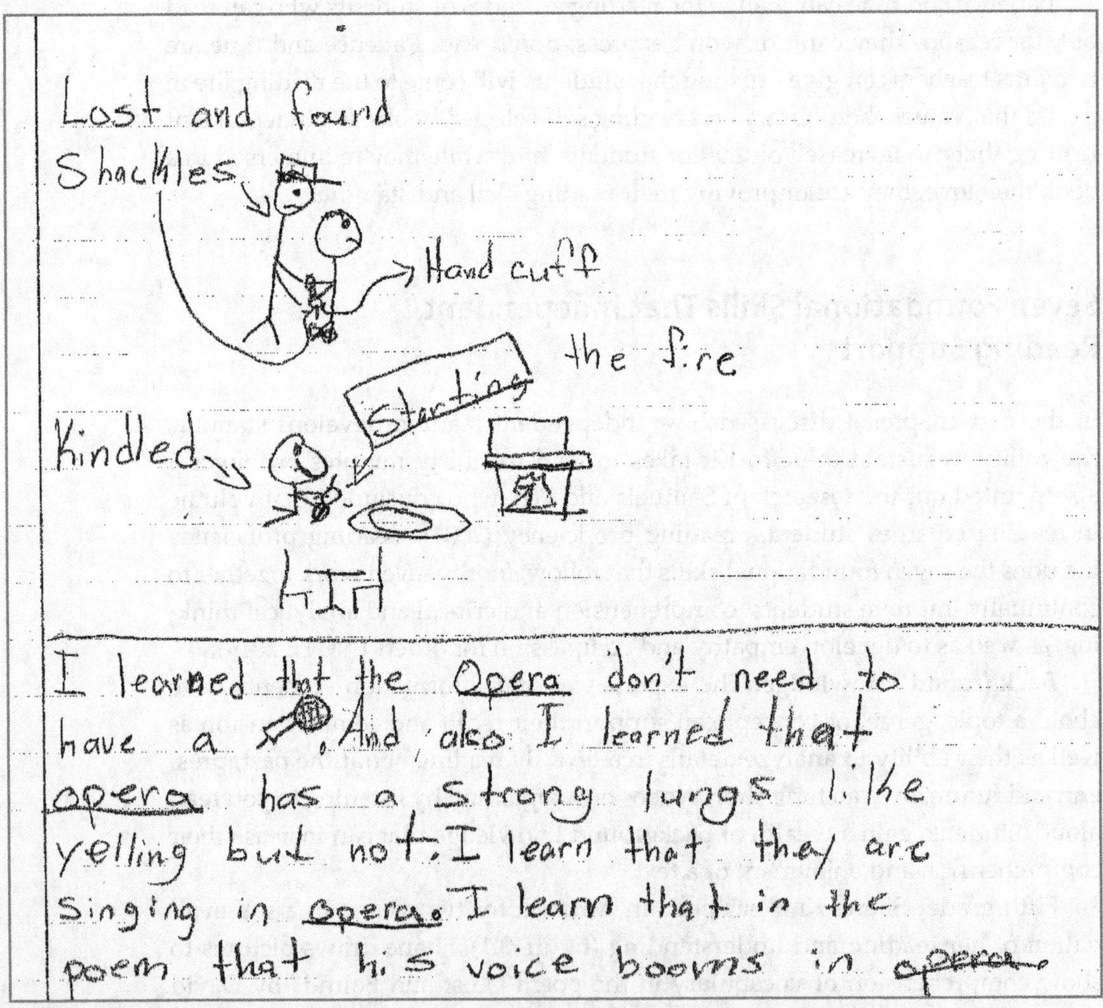

FIGURE 3.1. Shane Kim shows what she learned about opera singer Ryan Speedo Green.

words related to slavery and civil rights. When the teacher and I review students' lists, we find that twenty out of twenty-eight students wrote only four to six words. Before plunging into the unit, we decide to have students watch some videos and listen to teacher read-alouds in order to expand their vocabulary and knowledge of events leading up to and surrounding the Civil War. (The remaining eight students could choose to read articles and picture books the teacher and media specialist found for them.) Vocabulary also affects students' ability to think about a topic, discuss it with a partner or a small group, and write about it in their notebooks.

Fluency. According to Timothy Rasinski, fluency includes accuracy and automaticity in word recognition, and that means readers can decode but also say words effortlessly as they read. In addition, Rasinski points out that reading with expression is part of fluency and indicates comprehension (2020). When teachers read aloud, they model fluent, expressive reading. But Dr. Rasinski takes this modeling to another level when he recommends that teachers pause and point out how their tone of voice changes and how they slow down in parts or speak faster. The practice and ever-increasing volume that independent reading offers also improves students' reading fluency (Allington 2011, 2013; Garan and Devoogd 2008; Rasinski 2019).

Genre structure. Time for daily independent reading at school can develop students' understanding of how diverse genres work as they risk trying new genres based on teacher read-alouds and peer recommendations. Discussing books with partners, in small groups and conferring with a teacher can expose students to a range of genres, allowing them to figure out the similarities and differences among realistic, historical, science fiction, fantasy, mystery, thrillers, biography, memoir, informational texts, poetry, and so on.

Discussions. The desire to discuss a book and/or share favorite parts and illustrations with a peer partner and/or with a small group turns reading into a social experience (Robb 2017). Conversations can deepen students' understanding of characters and people and bond readers to books. First conversations are between the reader and the author, for while reading, students raise questions and make predictions and then read on to discover the author's position and to adjust their hunches (Rosenblatt 1983).

Discussions are oral texts that students create to share their thoughts about books. It's challenging for students to communicate ideas about reading: they need to recall specific text details and infer then clarify and organize their ideas into coherent sentences so others can understand their thinking. Discussions about reading also support students' understanding of literary elements and text structures and exposes them to diverse interpretations, allowing students to value ideas that differ from their own thinking (Newkirk 2014; Daniels 2002; Goldberg and Houser 2020; Robb 2017; Robb and Robb 2020).

Strategy application. During independent reading, students have multiple opportunities to practice inferring, visualizing, comparing and contrasting, and identifying themes and main ideas that students learn during instructional reading (Harvey and Goudvis 2007; Robb 2010, 2017). That's why daily reading of self-selected books at school can increase students' depth of thinking and diverse interpretations of texts.

Silent reading. By third grade, students on or close to grade level should be reading silently. This is an important goal, as reading texts out loud slows students down, and they don't develop their silent reading capacity. The daily practice that independent reading offers students can develop their in-the-head reading voices as they learn to read in meaningful phrases (Reutzel and Juth 2014).

As students' reading volume increases through daily independent reading, the seven foundational skills strengthen. You can support students' independent reading early in the school year by setting aside time to learn your students' interests and passions and develop a positive relationship with each one. Having this information enables you to suggest books they might enjoy, to order extra books for your class library, and to share students' suggestions with your school's media specialist so they can add books to the media center that reflect students' interests.

Interest Inventories: Know Your Readers

Before you invite students to complete an interest inventory, think aloud and "cold write" under a document camera to show how you respond. You not only model how to complete the inventory, but students also learn a lot about you. Here's my "cold writing" for three questions:

What do you enjoy doing most in your free time?

I love taking long walks, reading mysteries and thrillers, the Outlander *series, and watching movies.*

Do you have any hobbies? List a few and then write about your favorite.

I knit sweaters for the family, enjoy cooking and baking, and hiking in area national parks. Hiking and long, daily walks are favorites because it gives me quiet time to think—and best of all, it's relaxing!

When you're using a computer or handheld device, are you playing games, working on homework, visiting websites, emailing friends, reading blogs, or something else?

I write on the computer most days—I also use it to read articles about teaching. Read reviews of new books to bring to our class. Shop for books, clothes, read blogs, newspapers, email friends and schools.

Take a few minutes to field questions about your cold writing. Some students might write more if you permit bulleted lists, and it's helpful to make that part of your modeling. In Appendix A, Interest Inventory, on page 125, you'll find an interest inventory you can adapt to your needs. I suggest you have students complete it over two to three days; set aside fifteen to twenty minutes during each class to ensure their answers are thoughtful and detailed. Circulate among students as they complete the inventory and offer support and encouragement.

Interest inventories can help you develop trusting relationships with students, as long as you use them and show students you value the time they spend responding. Once you've read the inventories, schedule your first set of conferences to discuss them. Point out comments and information that show students how their experiences will relate to one or more of your reading units. As much as possible, connect students' interests to learning experiences and tailor your book talks to topics students want to learn about and enjoy. Surveys also provide information that helps you organize partnerships and small groups. For example, when selecting or ordering books for literature circles or book clubs, students' interest inventories can guide your purchases and offer them choices that engage and motivate them to read. You can also use students' favorite authors, topics, and genres to purchase new books for your class library.

Classroom Libraries: Daily Access to Books

Include books in your classroom library on different genres, diverse reading levels, and books that illustrate the diversity in our country. It's crucial for students to see themselves in books they read as well as to develop empathy and compassion by walking in the shoes of characters and people whose culture, religion, and lifestyle differ from theirs. A classroom library that includes culturally relevant books and reflects the diversity of the world invites students to learn about and experience the past, present, and future through books that can develop and nurture the empathetic global citizens that the future needs.

Students who have access to high quality class libraries read 50 to 60 percent more than students who don't (Ness et al., 4).

Students I've worked with (as well as other teachers) enjoy classroom libraries organized by genre

To collect students' suggestions for additions to a class library, you can have a box they drop their lists in or post a chart titled: "Books We'd Like to See in Our Class Library."

because that's how they like to find books. You can have books in plastic tubs labeled with a genre or you can label the shelves of bookcases by writing the genre on index cards and taping them to the appropriate shelves. In grades 5 and up, students can return completed books to the correct genre section before shopping for new books to read.

Invite students to suggest books, series, topics, and authors they'd like to see in the class library. Including students' voices and choices in book selection illustrates how much you value their input and moves from "my" to "our" library. Unsure about appropriateness of student suggested titles? Ask your media specialist or public librarian for help.

Too many middle and high school English classes don't have class libraries, and students only have access to books in the school's media center or public library. Here's a summary of what several tenth graders told me about class libraries:

"It's important to read in class because lots of us have jobs, home responsibilities, and lots of homework. That's why we need time to read books we choose at school."

It's the easy access, having books at your "fingertips" as Helena, a seventh grader told me. She added:

> "I check out books from the school library, but we only go twice a month. Our class library lets me check out books any day."

Independent Reading: Big Benefits for Students

Here's the bottom line: When you lobby for a schedule that has time for independent reading, time for students to practice and discover genres and authors they can't stop reading, they become better readers who choose to read for pleasure and to learn. Both NCTE and ILA have published documents to raise awareness of all children's right to read (Allington 2014; Krashen 2004; Miller and Sharp 2018; NCTE, 2018; ILA, 2018; Ripp 2017; Goldberg and Houser 2020; Robb and Robb 2020). As you read and reflect on the ten benefits independent reading offers your students, you'll come to understand why researchers and organizations like NCTE and ILA agree that it can and does improve students' reading skills, expertise, and desire to read, read, read!

Ten Ways Students Benefit from Independent Reading

1. Teaches students how to self-select "good fit" books they can and want to read.
2. Nurtures students' agency and literary tastes as they try different genres, authors, and topics and self-select books that interest them.
3. Strengthens reading stamina, students' ability to focus on reading for twenty minutes to one hour.
4. Improves fluency, reading rate, and ultimately comprehension.
5. Supports recall of information students read early in the text that they require to understand events later on, maintaining a high level of comprehension.
6. Develops students' imaginations as they visualize settings, what characters and people look like, conflicts, decisions, problems, interactions, etc.
7. Fosters empathy and compassion for others. As students step into the shoes of characters and people, they become emotionally involved with them and develop an understanding of other cultures and lifestyles.
8. Fine-tunes students' knowledge of visual literacy and interpreting illustrations and photographs while reading picture books and graphic texts.
9. Transfers students' passion for reading at school to the home and develops the reading volume needed to become proficient and advanced readers.
10. Nurtures pleasure and enjoyment, and when both these feelings are in play, students' desire to read more increases (Wilhelm et al. 2013). For students to choose to read outside of school, they must turn to books again and again because they're having fun, laughing, or feeling the excitement of learning new information and meeting new people.

Now, to address the elephant in the room: Assessing and grading independent reading.

Assessing Independent Reading

When teachers ask me, "How do I grade independent reading?" I always start the conversation by sharing two literacy snapshots: 1) A group of middle school ELA teachers went to their principal and asked him to do away with independent reading. All we do is grade projects on every book students read and it's too much for us to do, they noted. My response is to end book projects, as they punish students whose reading volume is high and remove pleasure from independent reading. 2) At a reading conference, a group of teachers and their superintendent asked to speak to me. The superintendent explained that this school year, he required students in all middle schools to write summaries in notebooks of their daily independent reading homework. The English department chair added, "After a month, students refused to complete nightly summaries, explaining that it made the reading a chore. We [teachers] agree with our students."

"It's a school rule," insisted the superintendent. For a moment my mind went blank, unable to find a reasonable response. Then, it came to me: "Can you show me *your* notebook of summaries for *your* reading?"

Silence—for what felt like an eternity.

"I never write summaries," he said.

"Then why have students complete nightly summaries?

"For a grade," he said.

Summarizing nightly independent reading also punishes students; it becomes an unwelcome task and removes the joy from reading a compelling book.

Researchers agree that independent reading is the one daily school experience that can boost *all* students' reading skill (Allington and McGill-Frazen 2021; Krashen 2004; Miller and Sharp 2018; Robb and Robb 2020). Below are five independent reading assessments that need to go because they're not authentic literacy experiences like the ways adults engage with books. Moreover, they can discourage students from reading self-selected books at school.

Five Independent Reading Assessments That Need to Go

Dioramas can be fun in primary grades, but they aren't a worthwhile assessment for middle and high school, where they're displayed without a student presentation that reflects critical thinking.

Book reports, usually long retellings, are a school-made product and not an authentic literary experience. In the real world, people write and read book reviews that evaluate a book's content and themes.

Parent's signatures required to prove a child completed independent reading homework shows a lack of trust in students and become an unnecessary burden for parents.

Summaries in notebooks are not what you, I, and other adults do while reading a book or after completing a book. As the superintendent honestly said: "It's for a grade," and that's a poor tradeoff for the negative associations with reading that nightly summaries produce.

A project for every book read is unreasonable for students and teachers. Moreover, it can force students to go underground with the number of books completed as a way to avoid extra work.

Independent Reading Assessment Snapshot

It's helpful for you to view independent reading as the glass half-full. Most students will be honest when they enter the title, author, and date completed or abandoned on a book log list (see Appendix I, Reading Log Form, on page 140 for a sample book log). Sure, there will be students who opt out of independent reading at home and list books they didn't read. Usually, one of two things happens:

- Students cave to the pressure of observing peers read, share books, and express their enjoyment. They start reading much like the protagonist in Bernard Malamud's short story, "A Summer's Reading."
- When teachers select a book from students' book log lists, one the student hasn't read, that's the time to have a positive discussion that places the solution on the student.

I usually select the book for the second or third book talk students present. That's when eighth grader Roger asks to see me during his lunch period. When he tells me he hasn't read any of the three books listed for October, I gently ask, "What do you suggest you do?"

Roger pauses for a minute or two and first tells me that he'll just take an F.

"Hmm," I say. "Is that your only choice?"

After a long pause, Roger says that he could read a book and then give a book talk.

"Now, *that* is an excellent suggestion. Let's look through the class library and find a book that's not too long, but one you want to read." I don't fail students, so that was not an option. The point is for Roger to read, and I count on him getting there. But I don't let my attention slip after he presents an excellent book talk that inspires three students to sign up for the book and causes me to praise his efforts in an email. We have several short conversations about the purpose of independent reading, about choosing books he could read with pleasure, about only listing books he has read, and about how his notebook writing shows great insights into character development and theme. Roger receives the "A" he deserves for his book talk. He and I continue to have frequent short conversations that show him I care, support his efforts, and take time to notice how well he is using independent reading class time.

Punishing Roger for being dishonest, not listening to and considering his suggestions, or giving him a zero for not completing an assignment would only raise his frustration and anger levels and send the message that I didn't care about his reading life.

I understand how difficult it is to shed teaching experiences used for several years—experiences that you had in middle and high school. I've been there! To help you toss these as quickly as trees lose their leaves on a windy autumn day, I've included four authentic independent reading experiences that also have the added benefit of advertising beloved books to all students. Remember, when students read five to ten books a month, it's not possible to assess each one—nor *should* you do this. You can assess one to two, but it's a matter of trusting that students did the reading.

Four Manageable Independent Reading Assessments That Students Enjoy

As you explore and reflect on the four independent reading assessments that follow, remember that there's no need to monitor every book students read.

Informal book shares are ungraded and can occur every six to eight weeks. The overarching purpose is for students to share a favorite book and why they enjoyed it or an abandoned book and why they decided not to complete it. Set aside ten minutes of a class, organize students into groups of four, and invite them to select a book to share from their reading log lists. Create different groupings each time students meet for book sharing. Ask students to have their notebooks ready to jot down titles of books they might want to browse through and check out. Browsing includes thinking about the title and cover, reading the back cover or inside book jacket notes, looking at illustrations, charts, and diagrams, and reading a few pages.

Peer book conferences work well once you have conferred a few times with students, and they have a mental model of the process. Students enjoy choosing a partner to confer with, and once pairs have completed their books, they can confer during independent reading. Students discuss different books and introduce peers to other reading possibilities. If they've read the same book, it's fine to confer about it. Conferences take two to three minutes, and students can respond to prompts/questions they select in their readers' notebooks or on separate paper. Sixth-grade students developed the form that follows, as I believe students should discuss what's meaningful to them (figure 3.2). You can grade some of their responses, but you'll need to establish criteria with them and let them know that you plan to grade their write-ups.

Book talks are short, take two to three minutes to present, and require thoughtful preparation. The best way for students to learn the art of book talking is to watch you book talk a completed read-aloud or a favorite book from the classroom library. The purpose of a book talk is to interest or disinterest others

Peer Book Conference Prompts/Questions

Directions: Choose two questions to discuss with your partner. When you've finished, head a page in your notebook, write each question, and under each one summarize the high points of your discussion. You can use bulleted jots as responses. Give examples from the book to support your thinking.

- Why did you choose this book?
- What about the book made you want to keep reading?
- Describe an event, character's decision, or setting that you related to and explain why.
- Did this person in your biography or this character in your novel face obstacles? Tell about two obstacles and how the person dealt with each one.
- Would you read another book by this author? Why?
- Who in our class would you recommend this book to? Why?
- Are there diagrams or photos you want to share? Choose two to three and explain why each meant something to you.
- Did you dislike anything about the book? Explain.
- How did your reading go? Were you into the book and didn't want to stop or did your mind wander? Explain why.
- What genre is the book? Is this a favorite or new genre for you? How do you feel about the genre? Would you read other books that are similar? Explain why.

FIGURE 3.2. Questions sixth-grade students developed for peer book conferences.

in reading the book. Show students how you plan a book talk by "cold writing" notes for your book talk on a 4″ × 6″ index card placed under a document camera. My notes for *Internment* by Samira Ahmed include a short summary and a quote from the book that resonated with me (figure 3.3). These help me build students' mental model of the planning process.

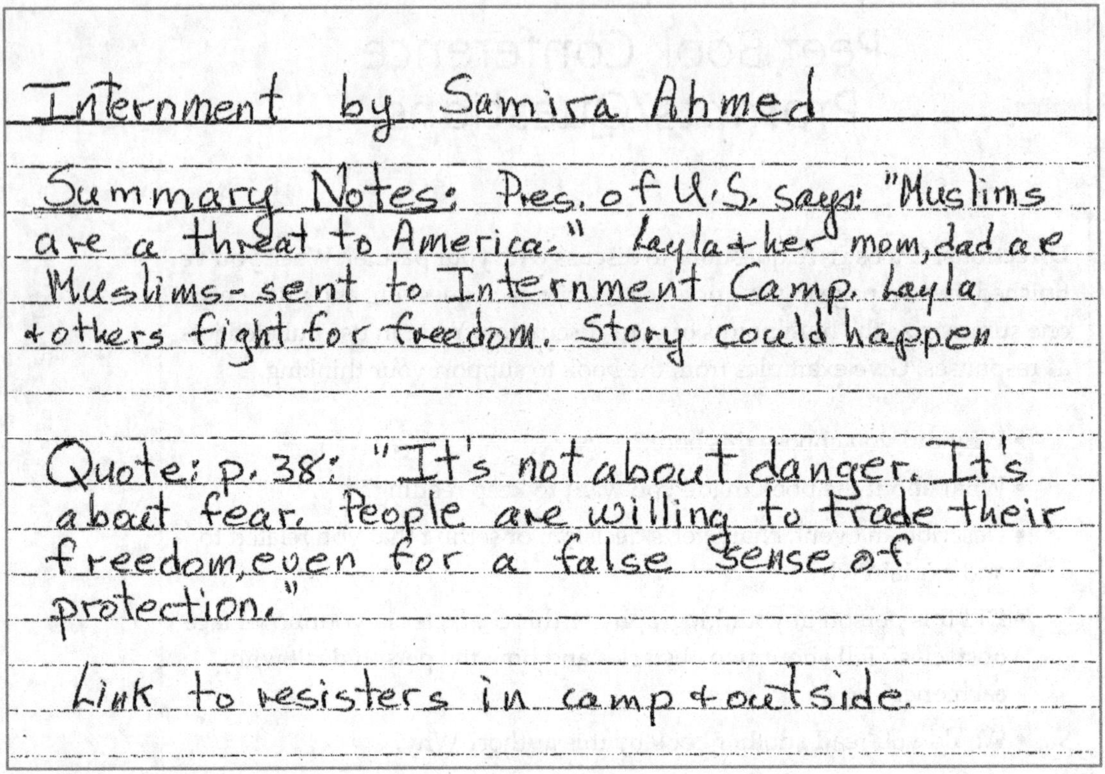

Internment by Samira Ahmed

Summary Notes: Pres. of U.S. says: "Muslims are a threat to America." Layla + her mom, dad are Muslims - sent to Internment Camp. Layla + others fight for freedom. Story could happen

Quote: p. 38: "It's not about danger. It's about fear. People are willing to trade their freedom, even for a false sense of protection."

Link to resisters in camp + outside.

FIGURE 3.3. The author's notes for a book talk on *Internment* by Samira Ahmed.

Before presenting the book talk for *Internment*, I share the cover and discuss the word "resist" on the girl's hat as well as the symbolism of the stars and moon, the black clothes, the red barbed wire, and blood-red title. Then I present my book talk.

Students and I discuss how notes on my index card were brief and that I elaborated on them as I book talked *Internment*. After responding to two questions, three students want to read the book. There are two copies in the class library plus my copy, allowing all three to read it at the same time. If you don't have multiple copies of a book, there's always the option of checking your school's media center or going to the public library.

> *It's great if schools can set aside extra funds to purchase multiple copies of popular books for your class library.*

Students should plan their first book talk during class, so you can answer questions and provide feedback. It's also helpful for students to practice presenting the book talk to a partner, so they get experience elaborating on the notes.

In my classes, students commit to a book talk each month. Sometimes I select a book from their list; most times they choose. You can set aside two days near the end of the month and have half the class present on each day. Or you can invite students to let you know when they're ready to present and sprinkle book talks throughout the week. When a class of twenty-five students share book talks each month, in ten months they will hear about 250 books. That data, combined with book talks you and the media specialist present, can introduce students to about 300 books a school year. Moreover, there's great power in peer-to-peer reading recommendations!

Book Talking Guidelines for Students

Book talks should raise the desire-to-read energy in a class, and it's important for students to discuss in small groups what they'd like to hear in a book talk. Possibilities are wide open with the exception of retelling the book, for giving away the plot of the entire book can remove the desire to read it. The goal is to leave listeners wondering, wanting to learn more, and eventually checking out the book. What follows are suggestions I've collected from students for many years. Feel free to use these but also consider sharing some with your students and inviting them to discuss ideas and add to the list. Offering students choices for the content of book talks invests them in the presenting and listening process.

Always remind students to bring the book and briefly share and discuss important points featured in the title and cover illustration. Open by stating the genre and a two to three sentence summary that piques peers' interest (see page 85 in chapter five). Never give away the ending.

Seven Student Ideas for Book Talks

Encourage students to explain why others would or wouldn't enjoy reading their book.

- Find a short quote from the book that spoke to you. Share the quote by writing it on a whiteboard, explain why it resonated with you, and describe how it connects to a theme in the book.
- Share a cliffhanger and how it made you feel and react. If the book has lots of cliffhangers, mention this in the book talk.
- Briefly retell a scary event in the book and what aroused your fears.

- Explain why your peers would want to read the book by citing a character you connected with or an event or decision that changed your thinking.
- Explain one way the book changed your thinking about the topic.
- Share why this was an I-can't-stop-reading-it book.
- Read aloud a scary, compelling, or controversial part and comment on the passage.
- Explain why you disliked the book and why you didn't abandon it.

Book Talking Suggestions for Teachers

If you don't have time to quick-read the book, you can read part of the first chapter out loud and/or share and discuss the cover illustration in order to interest students. Set aside class time to book talk a few new additions to the classroom library as well as authors and genres you're featuring. How you display books can be an invitation to students to browse through them. You can place books along the chalkboard tray or underneath it, on your desk and windowsills, or on top of bookshelves and filing cabinets. An abundance of books sends the message that books mean a lot to you—a message worth telegraphing again and again!

> **Book Trailers**
>
> Your tech-savvy students might prefer to create a book trailer as their book talk or book review. Students can explore book trailers on the YouTube channel (www.youtube.com/playlist?list=PL0A3EC21903A84659).

Book Reviews

Book reviews offer students opportunities to practice writing an authentic literary genre that enables readers to decide if the book interests them enough to read it. Before asking students to write a review, it's helpful to find book reviews to use as mentor texts so students can figure out how book reviews work. Check with your media specialist to see if your library subscribes to *The Horn Book* and/or *School Library Journal* and have pairs or small groups discuss a book review and collect basic elements. You can find students' book reviews and reviews from diverse sources by typing "student book reviews" into a search engine.

There are three parts to a book review: 1) a brief summary and defining the genre; 2) an evaluation of the book; and 3) a recommendation to your audience to read or skip the book in review.

Book Review Guidelines

Keep the review short: one page handwritten or three-quarters of a page typed double-spaced.

- Write your name and date at the top of the page.
- Skip a line and write the book's title, author, and ISBN number.
- Write a lead sentence that includes a short but compelling quote from the book or a sentence that compares the book to a movie or a related book. Then, write a brief summary (see pages 79 and 85 in chapter five).
- Evaluate the book. Let the reader know its strengths and weaknesses and support your ideas with brief examples from the book.
- Give the book a thumbs up or down with an explanation. Explain why you do or don't recommend the book by offering one to two specific reasons.

To help students write an evaluation of their book, share the questions that follow. Avoid limiting students to these criteria, but use them as a starting point to provide structure and guidelines for ELL students and developing readers.

You can invite students to write book reviews once each semester.

Questions and Prompts for Book Reviews: Nonfiction

1. Did you enjoy special nonfiction features? *Students can discuss information in sidebars and captions, unusual photographs, or excerpts from diaries, letters, and news articles.*
2. Was the writing interesting or boring? *Was it a challenge to concentrate on the reading? Did the author include stories that held your interest or helped you understand a difficult concept?*
3. What new understandings about history or the topic did you develop? *Discuss whether the book enlarged your knowledge of a topic such as the Everglades, drugs, the Industrial Revolution, or the Civil Rights Movement. Did the author change the way you view an historical event or a science topic, such as using animals to test cosmetics?*
4. How did you connect to and react to the life experiences of the person in the biography or memoir? What did you find fascinating about

their life and achievements? *Explain what this person did that changed the course of history, science, or others' lives. Does this person have characteristics you admire or dislike? Explain why. What decisions changed this person's life? How did other people and/or obstacles affect his/her life?*

5. Were photographs or illustrations effective? *Explain why these intrigued you. Did you learn information from them? Did you see things you never saw before?*

Questions and Prompts for Book Reviews: Fiction

1. Was the book a page-turner? Why or why not? *Show how the action or what happened, the character's problems and conflicts, or natural events kept the pace of the book exciting and made you want to continue to read. Did the plot contain twists and turns that held your interest?*
2. Was the story boring and difficult to concentrate on? *Discuss how the story contained very little action—nothing much happens in each chapter. Perhaps the plot didn't make sense—events weren't connected or events were presented that did not have much to do with the character's problems?*
3. Did you connect to one character, event, or conflict? Explain why. *How was the character like you? Do you have the same feelings, reactions, worries, problems, hopes, and dreams? Have you lived through similar events and reacted to them in similar ways?*
4. What new understandings about life and people in an historical period or dystopian world did you develop? *Did you learn how people behave and react during this time? Did you learn what life for children, adults, rich, poor, soldiers, etc., was like during this time period?*
5. Did you enjoy the fantasy world, the magic, and/or the protagonist's quest?
6. Why was the protagonist able to successfully complete the quest? *What was the fantasy world like? Did fantasy elements also include reality? Give examples.*

Post students book trailers and book reviews on your school's website for other students, staff, and parents to read. Students enjoy writing and sharing book reviews; Figures 3.4 and 3.5 show book reviews and self-evaluations by sixth grader Helena and by eleventh grader Lucas.

Helena H. March 25, 2020

Clean Getaway by Nic Stone

Scoob and his G'ma take a road trip together in a Winnebago. Scoob's happy to get away from his Dad's strict rules and disapproval, but has no idea where they're going. During the tip, Scoob learns a lot about his G'Ma, B'Pa, and dad and the Civil Rights Movement as they drive through the south. In the end, G'Ma brings her family together and changes Scoob's feelings about his Dad.

I chose this book because of the title and cover. It seemed like it would be exciting—and it was! Scoob learns about himself as he helps his G'Ma relive a trip she took with Jimmy, her husband before he went to jail. The trip was tough for Scoob's grandparents because his G'Ma is white and his G'Pa is black. A white woman married to a black man in the south meant lots of prejudice. lNow with Scoob, G'Ma is reliving the trip and trying to get to Mexico because she and Jimmy never got there. Scoob learns about Medgar Evers and places where people marched and stood up for civil rights and equality. Even today, some people in the south show their dislike for white and black together. Sometimes the plot felt slow. When the Amber Alert goes out for Scoob, and he hears it on G'Ma's phone, the plot races ahead and I had to read the book until I finished it. What I liked are the lessons G'Ma taught Scoob and his dad about trust and love and listening. And to thank her, Scoob insists that he and his dad make the same road trip G'Ma and Jimmy made and get to Mexico, where Scoob buries G'Ma's treasure chest in the sand.

Most of my friends and classmates would enjoy this book because it's about relationships and why it's important for family to stick together and help, not punish as Scoob felt his dad was doing. G'Ma has a huge affect on her son and grandson and the book can make others feel how important it is to love and learn from grandparents.

Self-Evaluation: for *Clean Getaway* by Nic Stone

I wrote 2 drafts of my book review and revised for meaning and punctuation. I followed the guidelines and put in text evidence but could probably have some more details. My summary doesn't give away the ending which really makes the road trip G'Ma took Scoob on even more exciting and amazing and courageous.

I would give myself an A-

FIGURE 3.4. Helena's book review of *Clean Getaway* and self-evaluation.

Lucas Hustick - Tuesday, March 31st, 2020

Columbine, by Dave Cullen - 978-0-446-55221-9

"Eric Harris wanted a prom date. Eric was a senior, about to leave Columbine High School forever. He was not about to be left out of the prime social event of his life. He really wanted a date." The narrative that the public is presented with regarding school shootings, generally follows a basic template. We are told that the perpetrators of these acts are loners, clearly mentally ill, and visibly depressed. In the book *Columbine,* written by Dave Cullen, Cullen challenges this narrative. Through his writing, Cullen encourages the reader to look past this stereotype, and to consider these horrible events as they truly happened.

One of the most important jobs of any book, is to simply tell a good story. While a message can be powerful, and the message of Columbine surely is, its delivery is contingent upon a well-told story. In his writing, Cullen does just that. He truly develops the characters, and effectively communicates to the readers what brought them to carry out such a horrible act. One of the most well written aspects of the story is the presentation of the idea that Eric and Dylan acted like any other kids. Cullen writes that "[Eric] walked right up to hotties at the mall. He won them over with quick wit, dazzling dimples, and a disarming smile." This strength is ultimately very useful to the furtherance of the overall point of the book- that the current lens which we view school shootings through, these characters of outsiders and loners, is ultimately not reflective of reality.

Continued on next page

FIGURE 3.5. Lucas's book review of *Columbine* and self-evaluation.

FIGURE 3.5. Continued.

The story of Columbine was undoubtedly a page turner, namely through its transition from chaos to order as the book progressed. As the book began, the structure of it was very chaotic, switching from perspective to perspective with no apparent pattern- an aspect of it which was emblematic of the chaos which surrounded the tragedy. However, as the book progressed and I began to learn more of the characters and events, it seemed as if an order rose from the disorder which Cullen originally created. Through this, I felt actively engaged with the book.

Another important aspect of Columbine is its impact upon my, and my classmates, thinking. Before I read this book, I felt very distanced from the tragedies that were school shootings. Hearing about them on the news, or over the radio, almost felt unreal- as if they weren't really happening. However, after reading Columbine, the notion that "anyone could do this" seems to ring much more true to me.

If I had to give myself a grade on this review, I would give myself a mid or low A. Ultimately, while I feel my analysis and adherence to guidelines was strong, I took much longer than I needed to write this. Also, I wrote one more paragraph than was required of me- however, I did so in order to preserve the clarity and integrity of the points I was making.

Closing Reflections: Collaborative Conversations

Discuss these questions with a colleague or at a team or department meeting.

- How does independent reading support students' reading growth and progress?
- Why should students share and advertise books they enjoy with their peers?
- How do book talks and book reviews promote independent reading?
- Why should you avoid assessing every book students read independently?

4 Extending the Reach of Partner and Small-Group Collaborations

Eighth-grade English teacher Resa Shelton has decided to introduce book clubs to her students. For the next five weeks, she'll replace students' fifteen minutes of independent reading of self-selected books with students selecting a realistic novel from five sets of culturally relevant books. Students' choices determine the book club they'll participate in. Shelton can do this because she plans her forty-five-minute classes over two weeks, and students have independent reading opportunities five times during that timeframe. Her schedule offers her the flexibility she prizes and allows her to do a variety of student collaborations during the school year. She can also block off several weeks of instructional reading time for writing about reading and creating and performing readers' theater and dramatic monologues. Before exploring the kinds of partner and small group learning you can manage in short class periods, it's helpful to consider instructional planning over a two-week time period.

Class Schedule: Planning Over Two Weeks

By thinking about your class schedule in two-week chunks, you can replace time reserved for independent and instructional reading with small group learning for four to five weeks. Doing this provides you with opportunities to invite students to have literary conversations and to plan projects that emerge from their reading. Note in my chart that I've reserved eight minutes each day for supporting students, so you can use this time to reteach or intervene based on your formative assessments (see figure 4.1). Catching students' confusions early enables them to move forward with applying strategies and skills. During this time, students not working with you can read a self-selected book or work on a project. (See pages 70–71 for more on supporting groups.)

Week One of Sample Class Schedule

Monday	Tuesday	Wednesday	Thursday	Friday
10 min.: Teacher reads aloud	10 min.: Teacher reads aloud	10 min.: Teacher reads aloud	10 min.: Teacher reads aloud	10 min.: Teacher reads aloud
15 min.: Independent reading of self-selected books	15 min.: Instructional reading	15 min.: Independent reading of self-selected books	15 min.: Instructional reading	15 min.: Independent reading of self-selected books
10 min.: Readers' notebook writing	10 min.: Partner/small group discussions	10 min.: Readers' notebook writing	10 min.: Partner/small group discussions	10 min.: Readers' notebook writing
8 min.: Meet with one or two small groups to offer support	8 min.: Meet with one or two small groups to offer support	8 min.: Meet with one or two small groups to offer support	8 min.: Meet with one or two small groups to offer support	8 min.: Meet with one or two small groups to offer support
2 min.: Wrap-up	2 min.: Wrap-up	2 min.: Wrap-up	2 min.: Wrap-up	2 min.: Wrap-up

Week Two of Sample Class Schedule

Monday	Tuesday	Wednesday	Thursday	Friday
10 min.: Teacher reads aloud	10 min.: Teacher reads aloud	10 min,: Teacher reads aloud	10 min.: Teacher reads aloud	10 min.: Teacher reads aloud
15 min.: Instructional reading	15 min.: Independent reading of self-selected books	15 min.: Instructional reading	15 min.: Independent reading of self-selected books	15 min.: Instructional reading
10 min.: Partner/small group discussions	10 min.: Readers' notebook writing	10 min.: Partner/small group discussions	10 min.: Readers' notebook writing	10 min.: Partner/small group discussions
8 min.: Meet with one or two small groups to offer support	8 min.: Meet with one or two small groups to offer support	8 min.: Meet with one-to-two small groups to offer support	8 min.: Meet with one or two small groups to offer support	8 min.: Meet with one or two small groups to offer support
2 min.: Wrap-up	2 min.: Wrap-up	2 min.: Wrap-up	2 min.: Wrap-up	2 min.: Wrap-up

FIGURE 4.1. Two-week schedule offering diverse teaching opportunities.

Trade-Offs Provide Teaching and Learning Flexibility

Thinking of your teaching schedule in two-week increments offers you opportunities for trade-offs, substituting small group work for several days during instructional or independent reading times. Here are four ways to juggle time within the schedule.

- On days you're not scheduling intervention and support conferences, you can confer with two students about a book they're currently reading.

- If you want to have more time for either notebook writing or small-group discussions, keep one of those activities running for two to four weeks.
- To schedule book club discussions, you can gain extra time by holding them during independent reading.
- To schedule alternate group activities that connect to either independent or instructional reading, determine how much time you'll need and adjust your schedule accordingly.

Daily read-alouds and small support groups should remain in your schedule because both are key to improving students' reading skill and progress and ultimately to developing students' love of reading as well as a personal reading life. Before you take a deep dive into organizing partners and small groups, set aside time to reflect on developing student agency through the power of negotiation.

Build Students' Decision-Making Power: Use Negotiation

A primary purpose of negotiation between teacher and students is to develop a classroom community that involves students in decisions affecting their learning (D'Agostino 2018). Negotiating with students offers countless opportunities to model helpful communication skills and build positive, trusting relationships. The fact that you include students in decisions shows them how much you value and respect their ideas. The skills students develop through negotiation will contribute to their success in future careers as they learn to listen to diverse points of view and come to consensus on issues. Here's a menu of what you can negotiate with students:

- Agreeing on deadline dates for work
- Developing projects related to studies
- Designing individual passion projects
- Discussing and deciding on choices such as teacher-led or student-led discussions; partner or small-group work; and additions to classroom libraries
- Using independent work time
- Setting personal goals and how to reach each one

- Setting behavior expectations for various learning experiences
- Deciding on formative assessments such as giving themselves a grade and defending it
- Finding ways to showcase their learning and progress through digital or paper portfolios; conferring; sharing with groups; and/or written self-evaluations

The amount of negotiation you and students do depends on your comfort level and desire to move to a shared learning environment and experiences. Negotiation brings students to the decision-making process and cultivates self-confidence and independence as students learn with a partner, small group, or on their own. The suggestions that follow for including small-group learning can be completed in two to five weeks.

Four Small-Group Learning Experiences

This is a pick-and-choose menu; there is no expectation for including all five in one year. Start with one to two the first year and then try out others once you're comfortable.

1. Book clubs offer students the opportunity to discuss in small groups culturally relevant books they've selected and truly want to read. Students can select different books connected by genre or theme and form small groups, or you can offer several sets of the same books just as Ms. Shelton did with her eighth-grade students (Cherry-Paul and Johansen 2019). It's important that books are at students' independent reading levels because they will be in charge of the reading and discussing (Cherry-Paul and Johansen 2019; Daniels 2002). Since this is a student-centered reading experience, it's best to introduce book clubs in the second or third semester after students have experience developing discussion questions and discussing and writing about texts. Students team up and do the following:

- Decide on the number of pages they can read each week and record schedules in their readers' notebooks.
- Complete the reading during independent reading time.
- Create open-ended, story-specific questions (see page 58) or use literary elements, especially when each student reads a different book. (See Appendix D on pages 128–130 for a list of literary elements.)

- Discuss each chunk of text using their questions and agree to offer text evidence to support their ideas, following the same routine for each chunk of completed text.

Try a variation on book clubs by inviting students to bring to their groups a book that they chose to read previously. You can ask students to choose a biography or fictional text and discuss differences and similarities in characters or persons, settings, conflicts, decisions, and outcomes, as well as how the book changed their thinking about people, relationships, and stereotypes. Students can also discuss the choices characters or persons made and how these choices affected them and others as well as why characters or persons changed and what caused the changes.

In addition, you can invite students to read and discuss informational texts they've selected earlier and share why they chose the book, what new information they learned, and whether the book changed how they think about the topic. They can explain whether the topic is still relevant and how the information has affected people's lives in their community, country, and globally.

You might want students to experience both kinds of books clubs and have them evaluate which they prefer, offering specific reasons. In addition, teach students to ask their own questions about a book. Such practice provides them with discussion prompts that are meaningful to them and develops in them the habit of asking questions while they're reading—questions that engage them with the text and nudge them to continue to read.

Tips for Developing Open-Ended Questions

An open-ended or interpretive question has two or more answers that can be defended with text evidence.

- Use terms such as why, how, compare and contrast, evaluate, assess, what & explain.
- Check to ensure there are two text-supported answers to your question.

Negotiate with students how you'll assess book clubs. Here are some student suggestions:

- Read and assess two or three notebook entries. Students can choose two questions or two literary elements they discussed and write about them. Allow students to select the entries you'll read and mark them with sticky notes.
- Let students create a checklist and complete it twice.
- Have groups develop a panel presentation about their book.
- Have groups "sell" their book to others, explaining why they should read it.

2. Teacher-led reading groups pull small groups for ten to fifteen minutes during instructional reading for you to assist students who require your expertise. Students not working with you can complete instructional reading, write about reading in their notebooks, or read their self-selected, independent reading books. Organize groups around common needs when students require extra practice on:

- Applying reading strategies such as inferring, determining importance, comparing/contrasting, identifying themes and main ideas, understanding conflicts, visualizing, etc.
- Engaging in discussions that ask them to cite text evidence to support their responses.
- Noting the reasons for characters/persons changing from the beginning to the middle to the end of a book or a short text.
- Completing short notebook entries about their instructional reading.

You might need two or three practice sessions with the same groups. Sometimes, you'll be able to work with two groups during the fifteen minutes allotted for instructional reading and other times only one group.

It's important to stop, support, and catch students before confusions increase. I find I frequently need two weeks, and then I return to my regular schedule; a few weeks later, I'm working with small groups again. There's no hard and fast rule regarding when you'll have to organize groups for interventions. It will be different all year long. The best advice I can offer is to follow your students' lead and support their needs as they arise. Intentionally scheduling this kind of intervention early in the year can positively affect students' ability to think with texts, and as the year moves forward, you'll find the need to meet with groups of students can diminish.

Keep records in a notebook of your work with groups. Write the date, topic, names of students, and who "gets it" and who needs additional practice. Having this brief log is your memory as you check back and reread your notes and wonder: *Why did they understand in October, but in March, the same strategy seems to be a challenge? Do I need feedback from my team for helping them find text evidence? Why is the writing in these students' notebooks still minimal?* Having clear and concise notes not only refreshes your memory, but it also contains information that enables you to plan differently and/or seek advice from others.

If you have to grade, then it's important to know that students will not understand your teaching or reteaching within the same timeframe. The goal is for everyone to understand the modeling, to think aloud, and to practice. Knowing this, it's reasonable to expect that once students "get it," they receive full credit for their learning.

3. Readers' theater scripts offer students opportunities to write and perform while sitting on chairs or stools in front of the class (Robb 2010). The time to write and perform a script can take up to two weeks, depending on the age group you teach. Groups can choose a completed independent reading book or a book club text and follow the guidelines below. Authors of readers' theater will have to cast characters and narrators in the script and have one to two rehearsals before the performance. Have students first show you the section in their book they plan to convert into a script before they develop one.

Writing a Reader's Theater Script

Guidelines for students

- Choose a passage in your text that has rich dialogue.
- Use the dialogue exactly as it's written in the text.
- Set up the dialogue the way writers do in plays:

  David: Maria:
- Place in parentheses directions for how actors should speak their lines:
- David: (shouting in anger) Maria: (whispering)
- Include two or more narrators. The narrator summarizes plot, setting, and descriptions between lines of dialogue in the text. Call these performers Narrator 1, Narrator 2, etc.
- Perform your readers' theater script while sitting on chairs or stools in front of the audience.
- Use tone of voice, facial expressions, and gestures to project characters' personalities and big ideas. There are no costumes; the audience visualizes and enjoys the work based on the performance.

Use the writing guidelines for a readers' theater script if you have to assign a grade.

After performing, the actors can lead a discussion with the audience using these prompts and questions and/or ones they compose themselves.

- Explain the feelings the performance raised and why these developed.
- What did you learn about the characters'/persons' personalities?

- How did the setting help you understand the characters'/persons' motivation and decisions?

4. Student-led literary conversations allow students to learn to converse with each other about their instructional reading. They are in control of these conversations because they create the questions, and this results in them accepting responsibility for thoughtful responses and maintaining the forward motion of the talk (Robb 2017). Book clubs are an excellent warm-up experience to literary conversations.

Guiding questions are open ended, have more than one interpretation, and can be used when students read different books connected by similar topics, issues and/or themes. They also work when students have read the same text (though discussions are richer with diverse texts). Guiding questions can open literary conversations. For a unit on discrimination, for example, sixth-grade students asked: *Why does segregation exist?* And ninth graders posed this guiding question for a unit on stereotyping: *Why does stereotyping limit a person's right to life, liberty, and the pursuit of happiness?*

Guiding questions are big and broad, and they invite students to dig into their texts to infer, analyze, and think critically so they can present evidence that supports their ideas.

By taking the time to teach students how to create guiding questions, you start them on the path to critical and analytical thinking.

Open-ended interpretative questions are another form of self-questioning. The research is clear: When you teach students to generate their own questions after reading, they can develop a deeper understanding of the text (Rothstein and Santana 2011; Zimmerman and Keene 2007). Since students must have a thorough knowledge of their text to create open-ended questions, their comprehension deepens as they return to parts, skim or reread, and then compose questions.

There are two types of questions: open-ended interpretive questions that have more than one answer and closed questions that have only one answer. For example, an open-ended question for *Clean Getaway* by Nic Stone is *Why*

Questions and Multiple Interpretations

Literary conversations encourage dissent among students, and this is important, for it reveals that the text can be seen from several perspectives as supported by the text evidence students provide. Encourage students to ask open-ended, high-level questions by modeling the process and then teaching students how to develop guiding and interpretive questions for texts they are reading. Both types of questions foster the analytical and critical thinking that can expose students to diverse interpretations of texts during discussions and can provide opportunities to value peers' ideas as well as disagree with them. In addition, by inviting students to defend in their notebooks their thinking about texts, you offer them opportunities to explore and discover their interpretations by using facts and inferences from texts to support their analysis.

does G'Ma need to take this road trip with Scoob? A closed question is *What is the Green Book?*

Have students work in teams when composing interpretative questions, whether they're reading the same or different books. Support from classmates can enable all students to develop the skill of writing questions that stir conversations about diverse ideas in their reading.

Getting Started: Provide a Mental Model with the Fishbowl

The fishbowl consists of two groups: a first group having a literary conversation and sitting in a circle and a second consisting of students who are observers gathered around the first group (Brozo, Frey, and Ivey 2006). Set aside the fifteen minutes of instructional reading for the discussion and use a short text (see Appendix F on pages 133–137 for two short texts) or a recently completed read-aloud. If you need extra time on the day of the fishbowl, take half of the independent reading time. Students read a short text carefully before they come to the circle.

Guidelines for a Fishbowl Conversation

- Set up the room with a circle of five to six chairs for students who will discuss the text.
- Establish observing purposes for students standing around the circle of chairs. You can group observers into teams watching the same element, and they can jot notes and questions in their notebook, but they remain silent during the entire conversation. Choose from these questions or ones based on your own situation: *Did the moderator keep the discussion moving forward? Did students ask interpretive questions? Did they listen carefully and respond to what a classmate said? Did they cite text evidence to support their ideas? Did they disagree politely? Were students respecting and valuing others' ideas? Did everyone contribute to the conversation?*
- Review guidelines: No need to raise hands—one person talks while others listen. Participants respond respectfully when they disagree. Encourage everyone to participate.
- Start the conversation by posing a guiding question you developed based on a read-aloud you recently completed or a short text that all students have read, including the observers.

- Encourage students to offer diverse interpretations. Explain that disagreeing with others' points of view indicates critical thinking as long as text evidence can back up the opposing ideas.
- Debrief the fishbowl discussion. Require that students not refer to peers by name but focus instead on the discussion. Suggest students offer responses to questions such as: *What did you notice about having a literary conversation? Did the conversation flow? Did peers use enough text evidence to convince you of their position? Were students polite? Did they value disagreement and a range of ideas?* Students' responses can support setting goals for the next conversations and also provide you with topics for mini-lessons and/or whole class discussions.

You might have to hold more than one fishbowl student-led conversation; continue until you observe students are ready to lead discussions on their own. As much as possible, include students in making decisions about preparation for conversations, notebook writing, and developing questions.

Negotiate Guidelines for Literary Conversations

Keep students in the loop and collaborate to set guidelines. By negotiating, you're inviting them to be responsible and invested in discussions. Here are guidelines eighth graders developed:

- Come prepared to the discussion. Complete the reading assignment and bring the text, your notebook, and a pencil.
- Collaborate with peers to compose open-ended questions about the text (if not using a teacher-assigned guiding question).
- Choose a moderator, whose job is to keep the discussion moving forward.
- Participate in the discussion, being respectful of others and their ideas, listening carefully, asking questions to help a speaker clarify an idea, and citing text evidence to support your points and inferences.

When students are ready to work in groups independently, have them use their instructional reading materials—students reading the same text converse together.

Important Reminders

Before student-led discussions begin, you and your students need to know what will be discussed. In addition, students need to compose interpretive questions, select a moderator who maintains the discussion's forward movement, and review the negotiated guidelines. Reserve one or two instructional reading times to accomplish this. Once students have had several practices, they will move into their conversations faster. The amount of instructional time you set aside for this depends on the length of texts or the number of chapters students discuss.

When you turn the process over to students, their first attempts will most likely be imperfect. That's the way it should be. Use debriefings to improve the process, and over time with practice, literary conversations will blossom. Your investment is so worthwhile as students learn how to:

- Collaborate and communicate
- Listen actively and respond to what peers say
- Develop open-ended questions
- Think deeply about a text
- Value dissent and disagreement and see them as learning opportunities
- Learn to respond to peers with respect
- Experience texts viewed in diverse ways
- Practice citing text evidence to support ideas
- Write in their notebooks
- Self-evaluate

Prompts That Keep Conversations Moving Forward

Make copies of these prompts and ask students to paste them into their notebooks and retrieve them during a discussion. It's helpful for them to practice the language of questioning and dissent with respect for their peers (Robb 2017). Eventually, and after much practice, students will internalize these prompts.

- So, we're supposed to [restate guiding or interpretive question].
- Does anyone have a different idea?
- Can you find evidence in the text that supports that?
- Is there more than one way to think about that?

- Can you explain that term?
- What points in the text support that claim?
- I'm unsure of your point. Can you clarify it?
- What made you say that? Can you give text evidence?
- Tell me more about that idea.
- Here's how I see that idea.
- Let's check the directions (or rubric).
- I agree with _______________ but disagree with _______________.

Here are some polite and respectful ways to disagree with a peer:

- I understand your idea, but I have a different interpretation.
- That's an interesting point I did not think of, but here's my idea.
- I find that idea interesting, but I'm not sure you can support it with text evidence.
- Even though our positions seem different, I believe they have common points. Let me explain.
- You proved your idea with text evidence. Let me share my idea, which differs from yours.
- It's okay to have more than one interpretation. Here's what I think.
- Your idea intrigues me, and I'm thinking my idea grows out of it. Let me explain.

Students debrief and self-evaluate with the checklist and/or by writing a short paragraph about their contributions and how the discussion went. (See Appendix B on page 126 for checklist.) Doing this is important because in fifteen minutes, you can listen to one to two conversations and complete a checklist (Robb 2017). By the end of two weeks, you should have listened to each group.

Avoid grading the first two to four conversations and wait until students are comfortable with the process. If your district requires you to assign a grade, consider having students give themselves a grade and then defend it.

After completing a series of literary conversations, you can also have students choose one or two interpretive questions, respond to each one in their notebooks or on separate paper, and invite them to assess it. You might want to

Checklist for Student-Led Conversations

Name 7th Grade Student **Date**__________

Directions: Reflect on your role in student-led discussions. Then use the key to mark the space at the left of each statement. Under "comments note extra details you feel are important to your self-evaluation.

KEY: N=Never S=Sometimes A=Always

PREPARATION

A Brings book and materials.
A Completes the reading.
A Helps develop discussion questions.

COMMENTS

I always finish my assignments.

PARTICIATION

S Listens without interrupting.
S Listens actively responding to peers' ideas.
A Contributes to the discussion.
S Respects different ideas and points of view.
A Recalls details to support ideas.
S Rereads a passage to support ideas.
S Asks meaningful questions.
A Keeps the discussion moving forward.

COMMENTS

Getting better at listening & not only thinking of my answer.

INTERPRETATION of TEXT

N Use pictures and photos to make a point.
A Discusses literary elements offering text examples.
S Uses text features to explore meanings.
N Refers to structural elements during discussions.
S Identifies themes and main ideas in texts.
A Makes logical inferences.
S Compares and contrasts literary elements.
S Compares and contrasts information.
A Makes inter-text connections.

COMMENTS

Additional Comments:

I want to do more use of pictures and photos and show how structure can affect meaning + help me understand more.

FIGURE 4.2. The checklist shows how a seventh grader assesses his participation in a student-led discussion.

model the process by "cold writing" a response to a read-aloud text and then reflect on a grade you would give yourself. With students, develop a chart of "look-fors" in responding to interpretive questions. One constant will be including text evidence to support inferring and thinking of interpretive questions that focus on:

- making logical inferences about characters, settings, and conflicts;
- showing what events, people, and inner thoughts caused the character or person to change;
- identifying themes; and
- explaining why the text changed your thinking about a topic.

As you observe partners and small groups learning together, you will identify students who require interventions such as support during short conferences or reteaching. Avoid delaying these supports. Instead, catch them early to maintain students' self-confidence and ability to collaborate with peers.

Interventions That Emerge from Observing Pairs and Groups in Action

You can develop on-the-spot interventions to help students who find a lesson challenging. Take a few minutes to review the two-week teaching schedule on page 55 and notice that each day ends with eight minutes for intervention, allowing time for you to support students' small confusions before they become large obstacles. There will be times when you won't need to meet with individuals, pairs, or small groups, or you'll only need to meet with them two to three times a week. It's the students' needs that determine the number of interventions.

High quality Tier 1 (core curriculum) instruction can support 80 percent of the student population, enabling them to show solid growth during the school year (Howard 2009; Tomlinson and Moon 2013; Owocki, 2010). Those eight minutes each day are precious because they provide the time for you to intervene quickly as needs arise.

Seventh-grade teacher Andy Rollins invites two students to join him at the conference table at the back of the room. After three days of modeling how to figure out characters' personality traits using his read-aloud "Seventh Grade" by Gary Soto, Mr. Rollins notices that Jon and Camilla have difficulty applying the strategy to "I'm Not Martin" by R. L. Stine, a short story both are reading. He's set aside five minutes to work with the pair and can continue doing this daily since he's reserved eight minutes at the end of each class. After modeling and thinking aloud on two consecutive days using characters' actions, words, and decisions, Mr. Rollins starts releasing the responsibility for inferring personality traits to both students. By Friday, Jon and Camilla are working together and supporting one another. They'll practice together and then try inferring personality traits independently. Daily formative assessments inform Mr. Rollins's interventions and adjustments to instruction.

The Value of Formative Assessments

When you're teaching and students are practicing, observe them, circulate among them, have a short chat, and determine whether you can repair a challenge on the spot in a few minutes or if you need to meet for five minutes over several days to move students forward.

As you circulate among students, you can gather daily formative assessments by kid-watching (Owocki and Goodman 2002; Wiliam 2017). Observe students during your daily read aloud and during both independent and instructional reading, while they discuss their reading in small groups and as they write in their notebooks. Unless you teach the same students throughout the day, it's not possible to read all notebook entries, so spot check as you move among students. If you want to see how students manage a specific response, such as comparing and contrasting two characters or different settings, invite them to complete it on separate paper, collect and read them, and then decide who requires support. When you return students' work, have them tape it into their notebooks so they have a record of all their writing about reading.

You can jot observations on the form that follows and keep these in a folder so you have a timeline of your observations and interventions. Note that I don't write something for every student—only those I feel require extra support. I follow up my work with students by jotting a few notes after I confer and students practice. Figure 4.3 shows my observations for one week. You can find a blank copy of the form in Appendix C, page 127.

Student's Name	Monday Date:	Tuesday Date:	Wednesday Date:	Thursday Date:	Friday Date:
Andy	Incomplete summary of his book. Needs support taking notes	Reviewed process on chart-we discussed benefits of notes	Talked thru each part of SWBS + I jotted notes—next time talk + Andy jots notes.		
Dolce		Checked out ind. read bk too dif. for her—says "All my friends are reading it."	Discuss benefits of reading a bk. She can enjoy. Offer her 3 bks. to browse + choose.		Dolce chooses Love That Dog. She settles into reading today. Follow up on Mon.
Frank					
Julia			Ind. Reading—Keeps choosing dif. bks. 3 today.	Confer to explore the why. Julia only wants horse bks. She's read them all in our library	Send her to media center after I chat w/librarian. Returns w/3 bks.
Keisha					
Max	Refuses to choose a poem from folder for fluency practice. Wants sports poem.		Offer him sports poems by Charles Smith. Now positive outlook		

FIGURE 4.3. The author's observations of students for one week.

What to Notice and Note

For each learning experience you offer students, here are some questions that can focus your observing and listening. This is not a definitive list, but it will provide you with suggestions to get started.

Instructional Reading

- Can the student choose books they can learn from and read?
- Does the student share thoughts with text evidence during partner and small-group discussions?
- Does the student attend during mini-lessons?
- Can the student use context clues to figure out word meanings?

Small-Group Discussions

- Does the student come prepared for discussions?
- Is the student an active listener?
- Are the student's contributions thoughtful and supported with text details?
- Does the student complete the self-evaluation form thoroughly?
- Does the student respect peer responses that differ from their own?
- Does the student value a wide range of interpretations?
- Can the student compose interpretive questions?

Readers' Notebook Entries

- Do notebook entries follow the teacher's directions and expectations?
- Does the student find writing ideas a challenge? Why?
- Do notebook entries reflect deep thinking along with text support of ideas?
- Can the student successfully complete an entry after the teacher models and thinks aloud using the teacher's notebook?
- Do a series of notebook entries reveal progress? How?

Keep your interventions under eight minutes. If students need more time then schedule them on consecutive days, gradually releasing responsibility to them until they can work independently. This invites you to focus your support, so instead of thinking, *I'll work on inferring*, the focus might be inferring to draw conclusions or inferring to identify a character's personality traits. A targeted intervention has a better chance for students to internalize a strategy or skill through repeated practice when they use the books, poems, and articles they're reading.

Short Intervention in Action

After the second time that sixth grader Jeremy is unable to discuss his book with Eddie, his reading partner, I decide to meet with both students to avoid the situation continuing and affecting Jeremy's self-confidence. I also believe Jeremy needs to hear how Eddie feels and work out a solution with his partner. "It's not fair," blurts Eddie. "I read and share, and Jeremy doesn't. I want to hear about Ted Williams. I love baseball. And he can hear about my biography of Muhammad Ali." Jeremy is silent. I say nothing, even though one minute of wait time feels like an eternity.

"Sorry," Jeremy says. "I like boxing and Ali."

Eddie says, "I'm the only one with a partner not sharing."

After a long pause, Jeremy asks, "Can I take the book home to catch up?"

I nod. The next day, Jeremy and Eddie have a conversation, sharing illustrations and parts of their books.

With pairs, sometimes it's best to let students share their feelings, as learning how a partner feels can result in positive outcomes. Make sure you're present during such an intervention so you can step in if negative behaviors arise.

If traditional solutions aren't creating changes, try to think out of the box when planning for these meetings. For example, when a ninth grader refuses to look back for specific evidence to support a point, his teacher pairs the student with a classmate who does scan for evidence. The teacher watches the pair take turns finding text evidence and offers positive feedback. For a few days, the teacher asks the pair to continue practicing.

When a student won't write in her notebook, the teacher asks her to retell what she and her partner discussed. The teacher writes what the student says and compliments the thinking. Soon, the teacher invites the student to complete her entry herself and returns to read it and praises her work. These sorts of brief interventions can "catch" students long before a behavior or attitude becomes an issue—and that's why they're important to students' learning and progress.

Closing Reflections: Collaborative Conversations

Discuss these questions with a colleague or at a team or department meeting.

- How can you adjust teaching practices to better use your time and offer students partner and small-group experiences?
- What can you learn about students by including teacher-led and student-led discussions about reading?
- How can formative assessments inform instruction and interventions?
- Why is it important to find time to intervene or reteach a lesson as soon as you notice confusions?

5

Increase Reading Volume: Instructional Reading Unit Libraries

For several years, I have been working in intermediate and middle schools with classes full of students who have instructional reading levels that span five to seven grade levels. Some schools require that teachers use a class novel while others use a basal reading program. When students reading below grade level can't read the novel, teachers accommodate by having them listen to the book and follow along in the text. There's no guarantee students listen or follow accurately, but the bottom line to remember is that they *aren't* reading. Annually, many in this group slide backward or make little to no progress due to lack of practice and volume in reading. In addition, one book for all doesn't support growth in students reading above grade level when a book and its concepts are an easy read.

Here's the good news: there is a way to reach students at diverse instructional levels (Afflerbach 2022; Fisher et al. 2020). With the support of your media specialist and reading resource teachers, you can develop instructional unit libraries that offer students choices, opportunities to increase their reading volume, have partner discussions, and write about reading in their readers' notebooks.

Developing Instructional Reading Unit Libraries

Organize instructional reading unit libraries by genre and theme (see examples in the box on page 74). When you immerse students in a genre for several weeks, you teach them to think deeply about and analyze texts, but you also help them understand genre structure. Having a solid knowledge of this enables students to navigate the genre and better understand themes and big ideas. It also deepens their knowledge of how the genre works—knowledge they can transfer to their writing, knowledge that provides them with choice of genres during writing workshop.

The reason I call these "unit libraries" is because each one contains ninety to 120 different books in a specific genre, depending on the number of students in your classes. Collaborate with the grades in your building to decide which genres you'll teach. Avoid repeating a genre until two school years have passed, so you have different books for students. In figure 5.1 that follows, I've listed several genres for you to consider. Some, such as essays, are more appropriate for high school students, so as you team with colleagues, keep two questions in mind: 1) Is the genre appropriate for the grade I teach?; and 2) Over three to four years, have students been exposed to most of these genres? One new genre for each of the four semesters offers you the flexibility to teach the genre for about six weeks but also have three-week mini-units on great speeches, magazines, and newspapers, as well as for students to rehearse and perform readers' theater scripts or short plays, develop multimedia projects, and to explore passion projects.

Whether ordering books or checking out books from libraries, it's necessary to have books for all the instructional reading levels you teach.

If your principal is on board with using a range of excellent genre books for instruction, the school might be able to find funds to purchase books for the initial genre instructional library as well as annual dollars to set aside in order to update the instructional libraries and replace worn books (Allington 2013; Robb and Robb 2020; Vaughn and Massey 2021). Your school's media specialist and reading resource teachers can help with book selection.

When I started teaching this way, there wasn't funding for instructional libraries, but I was able to gather books from my school's library and our community's public library. It's important to give busy librarians at least two to three weeks' notice for collecting books around a genre. Since you're checking

List of Genres to Consider

realistic fiction	historical fiction	science fiction and dystopian novels
folktales, folklore, legends	mythology	fantasy
fairy tales	biography	autobiography and memoir
informational texts	picture books	essays
short stories	graphic texts	drama
poetry	free-verse novels	mystery
newspapers (print and digital)	diaries, journals	thrillers, horror, and suspense
narrative nonfiction	magazines (print and digital)	speeches

FIGURE 5.1. Two-week schedule offering diverse teaching opportunities.

out books on your library card, avoid letting students take them home to read, as book loss can result in a large personal bill. Instructional reading occurs at school where you can monitor and support students.

Once you have the books for genre library units, organize them into three large color-coded plastic bins or cardboard cartons. In one plastic bin, place books for students reading two or more years below their grade level; in another, add books one year below or at grade level. Place books above grade level in a third bin. Only use color-coding on bins—not indications of reading levels. When you send students to a bin to select one to two books, you're offering them modified choices as you and librarians selected books you believed were age appropriate, culturally relevant, engaging, and worthy of meaningful discussions. The suggestions that follow will help with managing instructional unit libraries.

- Have students select two books in case one doesn't appeal to them or isn't a "good fit."
- Give students sticky notes and ask them to write their first and last name on the note before placing it on the book's inside cover. This makes retrieval easy, as students from other sections might be reading the same book.
- After completing instructional reading, students should return their books to the bin.

Storing books can become an issue, especially when each grade level has books for four units. The ideal place to house these instructional units is in a book room. This can be a room within your school's media center or a small room the principal can free up for storing books. You'll need shelving, and books can be organized by genre and grade level (Mulligan and Landrigan 2018).

ELA units will require the most shelving space. However, social studies and science teachers might have stacks of alternate books related to a topic—books students can read and learn from when the textbook is challenging. Label these books by grade, subject, and specific topic. Having books in a central place is beneficial because teachers will be sharing units by teaching them during different semesters. For example, if there are four ELA teachers, then each one will start the school year with a different instructional unit. By the end of the year, each teacher will have used all four different instructional units. It's helpful to discuss the order of teaching units before the school year starts, as each year might be different depending on the nature and needs of the new group of students. In addition, I suggest meeting about unit choices before starting each new one.

Teachers find that having five or six genre instructional unit libraries gives them more choices and flexibility. A goal could be to fund a fifth instructional library for the second year and a sixth one two years later.

If schools don't have the space for a book room, teachers can store one or two units on shelves or in cabinets in their classrooms. Each unit includes an anchor text that is your common teaching text. Teachers tend to prefer to keep these in their classrooms on a shelf or in a plastic crate near their desk.

Student Partnerships

Partners remain together for an entire book or an entire unit and are no more than one year apart in instructional reading levels, allowing them to have meaningful discussions and support one another. Some teachers prefer to keep partnerships throughout a unit or change them after students complete one or two books. You organize those student partnerships since you have the information that enables you to make decisions that support students' progress. It's best to try to resolve any doubts about pairs learning together before assigning partnerships. However, if one or both students object to working together, schedule a separate conference with each student to determine whether it's necessary to switch partners. Making changes at this point affects two other students who might be quite happy to learn together.

When every student reads a different book, forming partnerships has several advantages because pairs can:

- Discuss their books and connect them to teachers' read-aloud texts.
- Help each other with notebook writing.
- Become active listeners who respond to what their partner says.
- Support each other when learning new vocabulary and sets of words.
- Learn about other books they might want to read.
- Remind each other to cite text evidence to prove a point.
- Build their reading self-confidence through daily, positive interactions.

As pairs work together, you can circulate to listen, observe, and provide on-the-spot support to those who require it or decide which students need an intervention. Often, pairs want to read one another's books, and that works out well as both have gained the background knowledge to comprehend and enjoy each other's text.

For each instructional genre unit, you'll have to negotiate the number of books students will read and discuss with a partner. If the unit runs for six weeks out of a semester, then prior to negotiating the number of books to read and discuss, consider the nature of the learners in your class.

- Students who read three or more years below grade level need to read as much as possible. For example, you might negotiate that this group will discuss four books with partners but will read three to seven additional books during this time. Volume in reading will move them forward faster, and that's an important goal.
- Students close to or at grade level could read two or three books to discuss with their partners, but this depends on the length of the books they select. In addition, they might be able to read one extra book.
- Students reading above grade level can suggest to you the number of books they can read and discuss as well as additional books. Since they read well and widely, you can honor their expertise by inviting them to decide and then, if it's necessary, negotiate any changes.

The genre unit anchor text read-aloud, your common teaching text, provides the mental model and practice students need to succeed when discussing and writing about their own books (see pages 84–87). What you teach, model and think-aloud with the anchor text is what students practice with their instructional texts and what you assess. In the section that follows, you'll explore ways students can discuss different texts.

Ways to Discuss Different Texts

It's possible to have twenty-six students reading and discussing different realistic fiction texts (or any genre). In fact, I would argue this is preferable to one book for all because students learn about multiple texts they might want to explore, enlarge their background knowledge through discussions, and expand their knowledge of a genre.

Genre questions enable students to deepen their knowledge of how a genre works. For realistic fiction, students can discuss: *What about the protagonist is realistic? Do you feel the problems the protagonist faces are realistic and could happen today? Give examples from your book. In real life, events, decisions, and interactions with others change people: discuss how two of these changed the protagonist's personality, outlook, beliefs, values, self-image, and/or goals.*

Thematic questions have to do with ideas that are central to the story. To identify themes that run through most of a book, ask: *How does the title relate to an important theme? What was the author saying about family relationships or relationships among friends or with nature? Is there a theme that runs through every chapter in your book? What might the author want you to think about this theme?*

If you've attached a specific theme to a genre unit, such as obstacles for biography or warnings for science fiction, then students can discuss topics such as: *Choose three obstacles and explain how the protagonist or person overcame them. How did coping with obstacles shape the protagonist's or person's decisions, relationships, and goals? What in our world today was the author warning you about? Explain why. How does the author call your attention to specific warnings?*

Literary elements are structural elements of fiction, and discussing them can deepen students' understanding of their function in reading as well as in writing original texts. Students can discuss protagonists and their problems, antagonists and how each works against the protagonist, problems, decisions, relationships with others, etc. (See Appendix D on pages 128–130 for a list of literary elements.)

Conflicts exist in fiction and include these five:

- Person vs. Self: conflicts reside within the person's mind and emotions.
- Person vs. Person(s): conflicts are with other characters, their decisions, and problems.
- Person vs. Fate: conflicts that are beyond the person's control, such as being handicapped, suffering from a chronic disease, or being born with medical conditions such as cerebral palsy.
- Person vs. Society: conflicts are with institutions' rules and regulations, laws, school dress codes, honor codes, response to disasters, etc.
- Person vs. Nature: conflicts include natural disasters such as tornadoes, storms, weather conditions, settings, and relationships with wild animals.

You can invite students to select one to two conflicts that apply to their texts, discuss these, and then write about them in their notebooks.

Writing summaries can also be discussed. For example, use your anchor text to model how to write a summary. These are short and ask students to select specific details. Students need to practice this skill because summaries are part of book reviews and book talks.

In **summarizing fiction,** students can use Somebody-Wanted-But-So (see page 85) organizer, use their text to take notes, and turn those notes into sentences without giving away the book's ending (Macon et al. 1990).

In **summarizing nonfiction,** students can use who or what, when, how, and why and taking notes from the completed text for each word enables students to summarize informational texts.

To model and think aloud and then have students practice summarizing and different ways to discuss texts, you'll use the genre unit's anchor text and the teaching tools that follow.

Tools for Teaching with Genre Instructional Unit Libraries

In this section, you'll explore the teaching tools you can access to improve students' vocabulary, their ability to think deeply about texts, and their skill in writing about their reading in readers' notebooks. Besides an anchor text, you'll also need a large piece of lined chart or construction paper for an anchor chart.

The Anchor Text: Your Common Teaching Text

An anchor text is short and the same genre as your reading unit: a picture book, an excerpt from a long book, a fairy or folktale, a myth, a short story, a narrative poem, or a magazine or newspaper article. To model how to plan and deliver an anchor text lesson and make it interactive, I will use a short tale by the Brothers Grimm for a unit on folk and fairytales. The process is the same for any short text (Robb et al. 2023; Robb and Robb 2020).

Guidelines for Planning Anchor Text Lessons

- Read the text carefully.
- Use sticky notes to divide the text into teachable chunks. On the text, I've written STOP at the end of each chunk.
- Select one to two words to preteach for each chunk and make sure you include multiple forms of a word on the anchor chart. You might not need to teach words for some chunks. Try to choose words you feel students need for reading, thinking, communicating, and writing.
- For each chunk of text, create a few high-level questions with more than one answer. Put these on a sticky note on the last page of each chunk. Model how you respond to a few questions, offering text evidence. Then, remind students they need to give text evidence when they respond.
- Prepare your anchor chart. At the top, write the title and author, the words and sample sentences for vocabulary, and multiple forms of each

word. Set up the bottom and back of the T-Chart for student responses to what you are teaching, such as Inference/Text Evidence or Character's Personality Traits/Text Support (see figure 5.2 on page 81).

Anchor Text and Chart for "Grandmother's Table" by the Brothers Grimm

What follows is a short folktale by the Brothers Grimm that includes notes on how I divided the reading over three days and the discussion questions I asked students. Also included is the anchor chart for introducing vocabulary and recording students' responses. I can return to this text throughout the unit of study to model how I discuss questions with a partner, apply literary elements, infer, visualize, and model how I write notebook responses. For "Grandmother's Table" *inferring* is the reading strategy I model and partners practice.

Anchor Text

"Grandmother's Table" by the Brothers Grimm

Once there was a feeble old woman whose husband died and left her all alone, so she went to live with her son and his wife and their own little daughter. Every day the old woman's sight dimmed and her hearing grew worse, and sometimes at dinner her hands trembled so badly the peas rolled off her spoon or the soup ran from her cup. The son and his wife could not help but be annoyed at the way she spilled her meal all over the table. And one day, after she knocked over a glass of milk, they told each other that enough is enough. **STOP**

Discussion Questions: *Explain why the son and his wife were or were not justified in saying "enough is enough." Why don't the son and his wife understand the grandmother?*

They set up a small table for her in the corner next to the broom closet and made the old woman eat her meals there. She sat all alone, looking with tear-filled eyes across the room at the others. Sometimes they spoke to her while they ate, but usually it was to scold her for dropping a bowl or a fork.

One evening just before dinner, the little girl was busy playing on the floor with her building blocks, and her father asked her what she was making. "I'm building a little table for you and mother," she smiled, "so you can eat by yourselves in the corner someday when I get big." **STOP**

Discussion Questions: *Why doesn't the girl have negatives attached to separating her parents? How is this a story about segregation?*

Her parents sat staring at her for some time and then suddenly both began to cry. That night they led the old woman back to her place at the big table. From then on she ate with the rest of the family, and her son and his wife never seemed to mind a bit when she spilled food. **STOP**

Discussion Questions: *Why do the parents come to their senses? How is this a story about abuse and discrimination? What lessons did the son and his wife learn from their experiences?*

SAMPLE ANCHOR CHART

"Grandmother's Table"

Vocabulary: dimmed: dim, dimming dimmer
When the lights in the theater dimmed, the audience became quiet.
scold: scolding, scolded
Jill's mom scolds her daughter when she doesn't clean her room.
[Teacher models using context to figure out the meaning of dimmed and invites partners to do the same with scold.]

Day 1: Teacher thinks aloud and completes chart.

Inference	Text Evidence
1. Son and wife lack empathy.	1. They don't understand that she's not spilling things on purpose—she trembles.
2. They don't understand what happens to some with aging.	2. Son and his wife are annoyed when she knocks over glass of milk.
Day 2: Inferences students add during interactive lesson	
3. Grandmother feels isolated.	3. Her eyes filled with tears.
4. Son & wife are critical.	4. Most of time they scolded her for spilled food.
Day 3: Inferences students add during interactive lesson	
5. Girl's actions transform parents.	5. Both cry and bring grandmother back and don't mind her spilling food.

FIGURE 5.2. Anchor Chart for "Grandmother's Table."

The Anchor Text Supports Your Teaching and Students' Learning

Throughout each unit of study, you will return to the anchor text to think aloud and/or model ways to think about and respond to books. Use the anchor text to:

- Deepen students' knowledge of a genre.
- Model what sharing an instructional book with a partner looks like.
- Think aloud and show how to use context clues to figure out the meaning of unfamiliar words.
- Show students how illustrations, photographs, and text features can support comprehension.
- Model different ways to write about reading.
- Help students self-evaluate their notebook entries.
- Show students how to apply reading strategies to a text.
- Provide a model for responding to questions by citing text evidence.

- Teach literary elements, text structure, and the different types of conflicts.
- Offer students a model for planning and taking notes for an analytical paragraph and/or essay.
- Show students what taking notes looks like.
- Model how to organize journal responses with the anchor chart and your teachers' notebook.

In the section that follows, you'll find a detailed summary of anchor text lessons. You can refer to it as you plan and practice until you have absorbed the process by presenting several lessons. Anchor text lessons are your reading instruction and become interactive after you think aloud and model. If students can't apply the strategy, return to modeling and thinking aloud.

Guidelines for Presenting Anchor Text Lessons

Time: 15 minutes—if the lesson is 10–12 minutes after the first day, that's great.

First Day

- Name the title and author of the selection.
- Tell students what you will do, i.e., introduce vocabulary and name the reading strategy you'll practice.
- Pronounce the vocabulary word from the text. Use the word in an original sentence so it has the same meaning as the way it's used in the text. Read the original sentence you've written with the word in it and show the context clues in the sentence you've used to figure out its meaning.
- Read the other forms of the word. For example, "Here are other forms of perfect: *perfected*, past tense, *perfecting*, present progressive, and *perfection*, a noun meaning perfect. All words ending in '-tion' or '-sion' are nouns."
- Read the second vocabulary word and sentence out loud. Ask students to pair-share and figure out its meaning using context clues. Choose a student who volunteers to share their answer. Ask if other students have anything to add.
- Read the other forms of the words with a quick explanation similar to what you read for "perfect."

- Introduce the reading strategy and show how you'll organize your thinking on the anchor chart.
- Read aloud, pause to think aloud, and then show how you apply the strategy.
- Ask end-of-section questions. Remind students to provide text evidence to support their answers. If an answer lacks text evidence, ask the student to include it. Be student-focused and centered.
- Close the lesson with a *notice what I did*: refer to vocabulary and your application of the reading strategy that you write on the anchor chart.
- In an end-of-class wrap-up, note one to three things that the class or a group did well without naming students.

Second Day

- Quickly review vocabulary words from the first day.
- Introduce new vocabulary words and sentences. If students need more modeling, then think aloud with the first sentence.
- Have students pair-share and think aloud with the second sentence. Have students volunteer to share.
- Read all or part of the second section—project it onto a whiteboard using a document camera or your computer.
- Invite students to pair-share and find one inference in the text plus text evidence to support the inference.
- Students share while you write their responses (plus text evidence) on the chart paper.
- Ask end-of-section questions. Remind students to provide text evidence to support their answers. If an answer lacks text evidence, ask the student to include it. Be student-focused and centered.
- If there's time, you can discuss some of the other forms of the vocabulary words.

Third, Fourth, and Fifth Days: a Repeat Second Day

During the unit, try to incorporate all the forms of vocabulary words while speaking so students hear them many times.

Keep the Anchor Chart in students' view throughout the unit. It's a resource for students to use with their books and a reminder for you to review vocabulary words.

When Every Student Reads a Different Book: Organizing Partner Discussions

Now that you have explored a set of teaching tools that enable you to have each student read at their instructional levels, it's time to consider what partner reading and discussions look like once students have selected books. When students have a "good fit" instructional reading book, they can help each other chunk their texts into four to five parts.

Give each student four to five sticky notes, depending on the length of their texts. On each note, have students print: "Stop to Think." Next, ask pairs to divide their books into equal chunks of texts, always placing the sticky note at the end of a chapter or section. Then, negotiate how many instructional reading classes students will need to complete their first chunks. Since students will finish their first chunks at different times, those reading shorter texts can reread their text and begin their discussion, as they will be reading several shorter books to increase their reading volume while other students will be reading longer chunks of text. (They should also have the option to read their independent reading books.)

Managing Students' Instructional Reading

As students read chunks of text, they'll finish at different times. What follows are suggestions that enable you to evaluate students' book choices.

- Work with students to figure out how much time they'll need to read the first chunk. You can adjust if needed. It's important for students to be able to figure this out. They will get better with practice.
- Have students raise their hands as they finish the first chunk. Work with one student at a time, and ask them to tell you as many details as they can. If students can't, have them reread several pages and follow the same approach again. If students still can't retell with details, gently suggest they find another book—help them by giving them a choice between two or three books.
- If students can retell, remind them that rereading is a great strategy for them to use to recall those details.

As students will finish each chunk at different times, those who finish early can go to their independent reading book, which should always be handy on their desks. Then you can have students start partner work when everyone has finished a chunk (with the exception of developing readers, who will read several short books).

Taking Deep Dives into Each Chunk of Text

The "Stop to Think" includes students' jotting notes, discussing their books, and then completing notebook entries (Dorn and Soffos 2005; Robb et al. 2023). This occurs over a few classes during time normally reserved for instructional reading. Students' understanding will deepen as they think, discuss, and write about issues and central ideas in their books with a partner. Circulate among the students and support them as they progress.

The Pair-Shares Partners Complete after Reading Each Chunk of Text

When students complete each chunk, their first paired discussion of the chunk is sharing a short summary of what they've read. This keeps partners abreast of the plot or information in their books and makes their discussions more meaningful.

Show Students How to Take Notes for Summarizing

Using the anchor text for folk and fairytales, "Grandmother's Table" by the Brothers Grimm (or a text you've chosen), show students how you take notes for summarizing the first chunk before presenting an oral summary. Project the entry onto a whiteboard using a document camera and think aloud as you "cold write."

Somebody: the grandmother

Wanted: went to live with her son's family and after her husband died.

But: the old lady had poor eyesight and trembling hands; she spilled food and one day knocked over a glass of milk

So: the son and his wife said, "enough is enough"

Use Notes to Model an Oral Summary: Next, show students how you develop an oral summary using your notes. Here's what I say: *Because she's been alone since her husband died, the son and his wife invited the grandmother to live with them. Soon her eyesight weakened and her hands trembled, causing her to spill food on the table during meals. The day the old woman knocked over a glass of milk, the son and his wife said, "enough is enough."*

Now invite students to add a page in their notebooks that includes the title of their book and their summary notes. Keep your notebook model using "Grandmother's Table" under the document camera so it projects onto a whiteboard and is a resource for students.

Partner Discussions for First Chunk: Set aside ten to fifteen minutes each day for students to share and discuss. Encourage students to ask questions each time you model, as their questions and your responses can support their learning. You provide the model with the anchor text, and students find similar examples in the book they're reading.

- First share: Students take summary notes then share their summaries.
- Second share: Review using the anchor chart for "Grandmother's Table" (or any other anchor text) how you organized inferences and text evidence on a T-Chart.

Next, invite students to set up a T-Chart on a notebook page, write one inference, and then supply text evidence for their inference about a character.

- Third share: Review literary elements with students and think aloud to show how you identify the protagonist and that character's problem as well as identify the antagonists and how each one works against the protagonist. Here's what I say for "Grandmother's Table": *The protagonist is the old woman, and her problem is that her trembling and poor eyesight cause her to spill food during meals. At this point in the story, the old woman's infirmities are antagonists, and she can't control them and stop spilling food.*

Have students indicate in their notebooks the protagonist from their texts, their problem, one antagonist, how that antagonist works against the protagonist, and then share with their partner.

Partner Discussions for Subsequent Chunks of Text

Follow the pattern established for the first chunk of texts after students finish reading each chunk. Remember, what you modeled with the anchor text is what you have students practice with their instructional reading books. Here's a brief recap of your role during partner work:

- Model taking summary notes for each chunk of the anchor text. Take notes in your notebook, placed under a document camera and projected onto a whiteboard, so students can observe.
- Repeat an oral summary of your notes only if you feel students require this repetition.
- Return to the anchor text and anchor chart to model how you applied a strategy, used context clues to figure out words' meanings, applied specific literary terms, etc. As your common text, the anchor text becomes a powerful teaching tool for you and an equally powerful learning experience for your students.

- Reserve time for students to ask questions after you model.
- As students complete discussions and notebook work, circulate and support them.

When Students Are Halfway through Their Books

This is a good time to reflect on students' discussions, notebook writing, and your observations. If most of the class shows you they are ready for you to do so, you can introduce another reading strategy, showcase a new literary element, or have students discuss relationships (or other themes that go with a genre) they have already observed.

Students' Second Book and Beyond

During an instructional genre-based unit, partners will collaborate on two to four books. Follow the same process outlined for the first book. If most students require more practice with a strategy, note that on your unit plan (see Appendix E on pages 131–132 for more on unit plans). Also record on your plan any adjustments you made as students read the second and third books. Base your teaching decisions on what students show you, noting what they understand as well as areas where they need more practice. Support for instructional decisions can come from students' questions, discussions, notebook writing, your observations, and conference notes.

Notes and discussions that follow sharing a summary depend on what's been modeled with the anchor text and chart and in your teachers' notebook. This can include conflicts, literary elements, text structures and features, genre- and theme-based questions, and using context clues to figure out unfamiliar words, as well as planning and composing an analytical paragraph and essay. With the exception of preparing and sharing summaries, partner discussions precede completing notebook entries, as talk stirs reflection and synthesizing ideas while teachers' notebooks provide expectations and models of writing about reading.

Teachers' Notebooks

Your anchor text and teachers' notebook are the teaching tools you'll use again and again to build students' mental models of how to apply a strategy, find themes and main ideas, and write about reading. If you have a document camera, you can place your notebook under it, and "cold write" in front of students projecting your "cold write" onto a whiteboard. You can keep your teachers' notebook online if you don't have access to a document camera and instead project what you're writing onto a whiteboard.

It's beneficial for students to observe you "cold write" because they see that planning and drafting aren't perfect. You'll have opportunities to cross out ideas you want to rewrite or eliminate (Crowder 2020). Though not exhaustive, the list that follows shows the kind of modeling you can do in your notebook.

- Summarizing fiction and nonfiction.
- Writing quick responses to reading, such as lists of words that describe a character, words that reveal emotional responses, explaining why events connect, and questions the text raises.
- Applying reading strategies such as inferring, visualizing, drawing conclusions, identifying personality traits, determining importance, etc.
- Using context to explain vocabulary.
- Showing how characters change from the beginning to the end of a story.
- Noting themes in a novel and informational text.
- Identifying main ideas.
- Following a character or person and commenting on their decisions, reactions, interactions, inner thoughts, conflicts, etc.
- Planning an analytical paragraph and essay (see Appendixes J and K on pages 141–144).

Seeing your thinking and writing processes can help students complete a similar response because they have a model and a resource they can look at if they need review. Teachers I work with keep their notebooks in a place that's accessible to students, who are free to review and reread specific entries. What follows is the "cold write" from my notebook for an eighth-grade class on the question, *How has the book you've completed changed your thinking? Explain why or why not* (figure 5.3). The text I used was a recent read aloud: "Eyes Do More Than See" by Isaac Asimov.

Students' Notebooks

So, why have students keep readers' notebooks? My hope is that students will view their notebooks as their personal reading journey and record of their feelings, thoughts, and reflections about the reading they did throughout the year

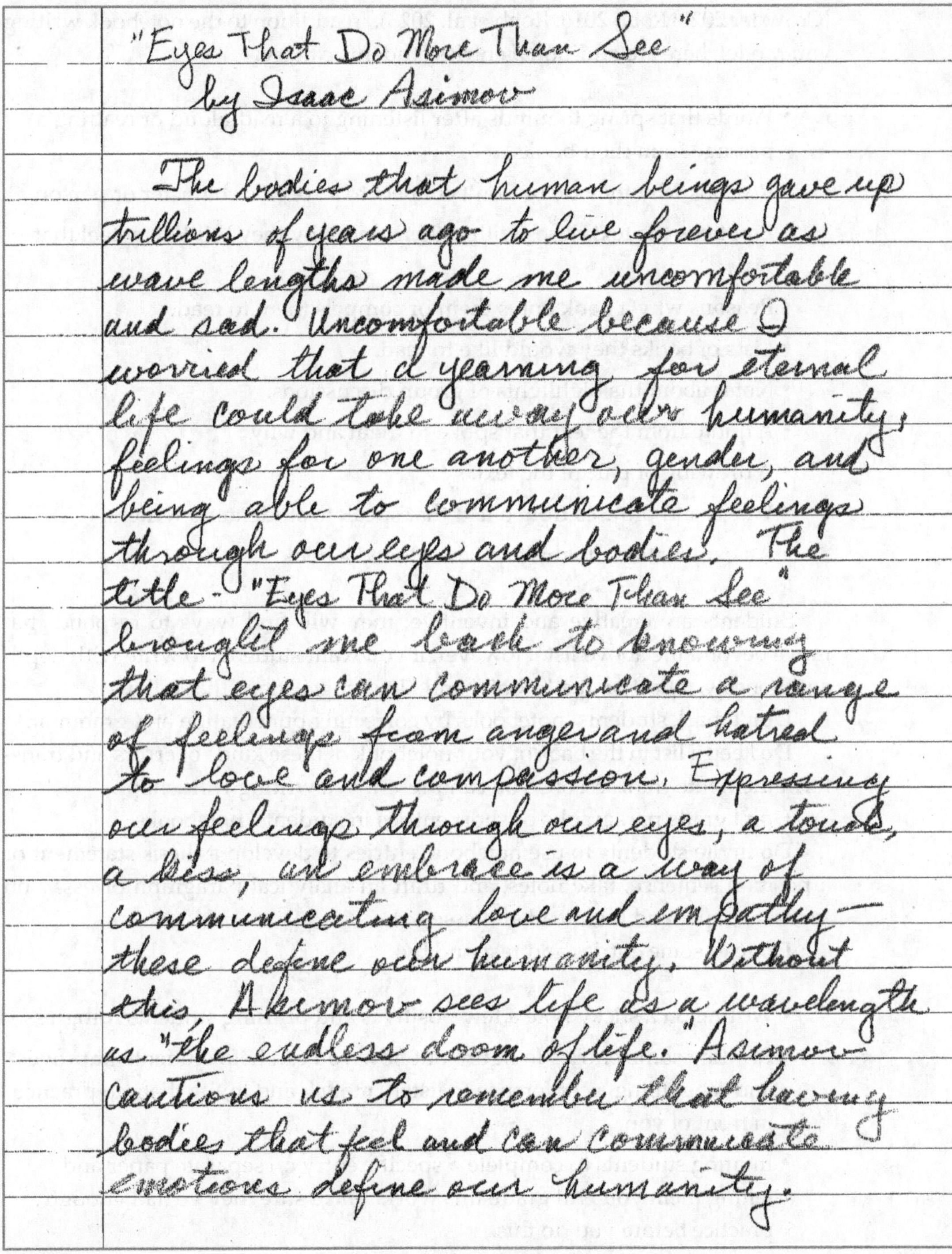

"Eyes That Do More Than See"
by Isaac Asimov

The bodies that human beings gave up trillions of years ago to live forever as wave lengths made me uncomfortable and sad. Uncomfortable because I worried that a yearning for eternal life could take away our humanity, feelings for one another, gender, and being able to communicate feelings through our eyes and bodies. The title "Eyes That Do More Than See" brought me back to knowing that eyes can communicate a range of feelings from anger and hatred to love and compassion. Expressing our feelings through our eyes, a touch, a kiss, an embrace is a way of communicating love and empathy—these define our humanity. Without this, Asimov sees life as a wavelength as "the endless doom of life." Asimov cautions us to remember that having bodies that feel and can communicate emotions define our humanity.

FIGURE 5.3. "Cold write" from author's notebook explaining how "Eyes Do More Than See" changed her thinking.

(Crowder 2020; Robb 2016; Robb et al. 2023). In addition to the notebook writing you model, here are additional entries students can try:

- Words that spring to minds after listening to a read-aloud or reading a passage from their books.
- Reasons why they do or don't connect to a specific character or person.
- Emotions the text raises within them and why they think they feel that way.
- Reasons why a book bores them or compels them to read.
- Lists of books they would like to read.
- Notes about the highlights of group discussions.
- A quote from the text that spoke to them and why.
- A drawing of part of the text.
- Words and phrases from a text that speak to students as writers.
- An explanation of why they abandoned a book.

Students are creative and inventive; they will find ways to respond that move beyond the above list. However, if you want students to write with depth and honesty, reflect on the "Don't" and "Do" suggestions that follow.

Don't mark students' notebooks by correcting punctuation and grammar.

Do keep a list in the back of your notebook of these kinds of errors and transform them into mini-lessons you can present in a writing workshop.

Don't grade paragraphs or short entries in students' notebooks.

Do invite students to use notebook entries to develop a thesis statement or a position sentence, take notes, and draft an analytical paragraph or essay on separate paper and then read and assess it.

Do read some entries and respond by:

- Writing on a sticky note a few positives and praising students' progress.
- Reading some entries to figure out how you can help students improve and scheduling a conference to listen, model, and invite them to practice in front of you.
- Inviting students to complete a specific entry on separate paper and telling them you will grade this work. Make sure they've had enough practice before you do this.

To read every student entry is an impossible task and one that won't necessarily support your teaching and students' learning. Instead, circulate as students write in their notebooks and read their entries, answer questions, and offer on-the-spot support.

Students' Book Discussions Lead to Deeper Notebook Writing

When notebook writing occurs after students have discussed a text with a partner or in a small group, it's easier for them to write. Students tell me that the ideas flow onto the paper faster after talking. They also point out that the talk generates new ideas and extends their original thoughts.

Fifth grader Avi discusses with his group specific sections of James Clavell's *The Children's Story*. Figure 5.4 reveals Avi's honest, emotional reaction to the new teacher cutting up the American flag. Strong, fearful feelings often bond readers to books. In this case, it did. Avi's response to two questions I posed that he discussed with his group reflect the effort he put into comprehending the story, his concerns about brainwashing, and the lies the new teacher told the children (figure 5.5). He gets the big point of the book when he writes: "It is easy to get little kids to belive what you belive."

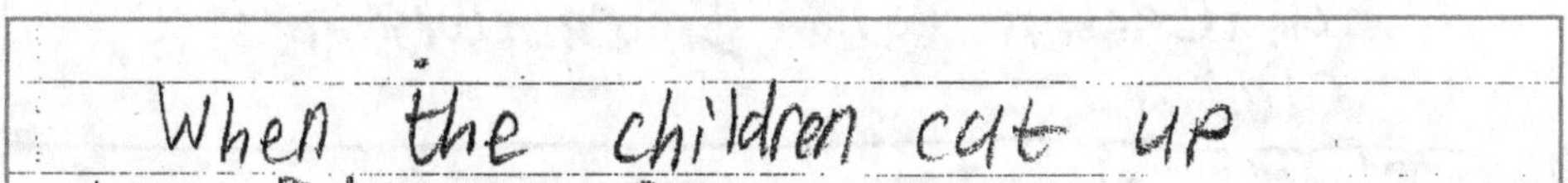

When the children cut up the flag, I felt like that was not a very good thing to do. When they say the pledge of alligence, you look at the flag. If you cut up the flag, there will be no flag to say the pledge of alligence to. When the author said they were going to cut up the flag, I felt an Oh No felling inside.

FIGURE 5.4. Fifth grader Avi's feelings toward the teacher cutting up the American flag.

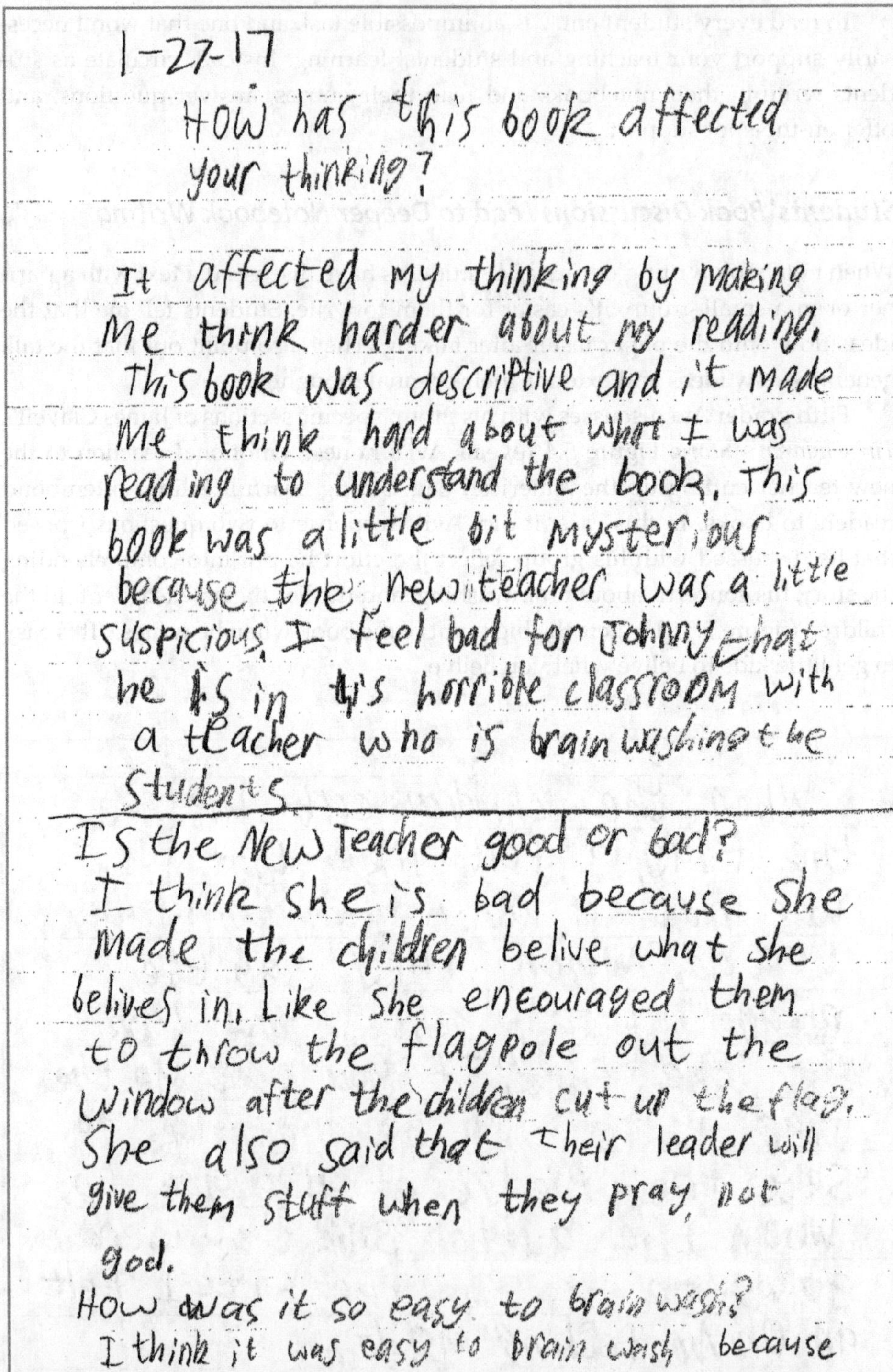

1-27-17

How has this book affected your thinking?

It affected my thinking by making me think harder about my reading. this book was descriptive and it made me think hard about what I was reading to understand the book. This book was a little bit mysterious because the new teacher was a little suspicious. I feel bad for Johnny that he is in this horrible classroom with a teacher who is brain washing the students

Is the New Teacher good or bad?

I think she is bad because she made the children belive what she belives in. Like she encouraged them to throw the flagpole out the window after the children cut up the flag. She also said that their leader will give them stuff when they pray, not god.

How was it so easy to brain wash?

I think it was easy to brain wash because

FIGURE 5.5. Avi explains how *The Children's Story* by James Clavell affected his thinking.

Eleventh grader Lucas and his classmates have read and discussed Khaled Hosseini's *The Kite Runner.* Lucas selects a prompt that asks him to discuss the ending of the story. To do this effectively, he returns to two resolutions in the book that support his evaluation of the ending (figure 5.6). His notebook entry reflects the kinds of discussions his group had and the depth of thinking and understanding that talking followed by writing about reading can reveal.

Notebook entries show students' interactions with texts and growth in their ability to express how powerful texts affect their emotions, and writing about reading can lead to a deeper understanding of the text. Students can self-evaluate their notebooks, and teachers can evaluate several entries. Teachers can also use several entries from students' notebooks to assess their growth or have them complete a specific type of entry on separate paper for assessment.

> Over the course of the book, there are two memorable resolutions (not including the ending). The first big resolution to occur in the book is between Baba and Amir, following Amir's kite flying success. We can see this on page 69, where Hosseini writes "It happened just the way I'd imagined" (69). Sadly, this happy ending didn't stay happy, with Hosseini writing on page 73, "getting sick" (73). Ultimately, what this evanescence amounts to is not much of a resolution at all.
>
> The second of the super memorable resolutions to occur takes place between Rahim Khan and Amir. It begins, again, with happiness—on page 172, Rahim Khan exclaims "It's wonderfully strange to see you as a grown man." However, these good feelings do not last long. A couple of pages later, on page 175, Rahim Khan says "Dying, actually" (172).
>
> It seems, then, that *The Kite Runner* does not have a track record of largely happy endings. In fact, it seems to consist of resolutions that go just far enough to resolve the conflict at hand, but not any further. In the same way, the ending of the book fits within this pattern. It does not at all come close to a glorious close, marked by the warm embrace between Sohrab and Amir- but it is a start, and it represents an end to the silence between Sohrab and Amir. In this way, it is very similar to the other resolutions which take place in the book, making it consistent with the story and therefore appropriate.
>
> To best determine what message the reader is expected to grasp from the end of the book, we must first acknowledge the perspective from which Hosseini writes the book. It would not be a far-fetched claim to say that Hosseini does not write this book from an idealistic perspective. Many times in the book, it seems, Hosseini critiques those who look at the world through an idealistic lens. The best example of this occurs on page 204, where Farid says that "That's the real Afghanistan" (204). In this sense, Farid shows Amir that the way he saw Afghanistan in the past- was unreal. Diving deeper into this, Hosseini, through the mouth of Farid, is telling the reader that the world is not as amazing as we might view it through our own eyes.
>
> So what does this tell us? Essentially, from this, we can infer that Hosseini is writing the book from a realist point of view. In this sense, we can look at the ending as nothing more than another premise in Hosseini's argument for realism—that it serves no other purpose than to show that life is hard, and there is no reason to expect some sort of magical happy ending.

FIGURE 5.6. Digital notebook entry by eleventh grader Lucas.

Assessing Instructional Reading

When planning assessments, it's important to remember this: what you teach with the anchor text is what students practice and what you assess. By keeping that in mind, you'll most likely be assessing students' understandings of:

1. Specific reading strategies. Look for students' ability to apply strategies such as inferring, drawing conclusions, comparing and contrasting, and visualizing to their text and cite evidence that supports their thinking.
2. The genre they're reading. Listen to discussions and ask students to write about what they've learned about a genre's structure.
3. Texts through their conversations. These can focus on literary elements, specific conflicts, informational text structures and text features, and students' emotional reactions to the text.
4. Texts through notebook writing. Students can show their understanding of any of the elements in number three above by writing about them in their notebooks and linking each item to specific text details.
5. Texts through conferring. You can use conferences to have students show you their understanding of any of the above.

Students' notebook writing can enable you to assess their writing about reading and provide you with a window into their thinking. If you organize your teaching into reading units of study, you can develop rubrics that let students know your expectations for notebook writing about reading.

Developing Assessment Rubrics

Wanda Waters, a fifth-grade teacher who works with English language learners and students arriving in her fifth-grade classes reading at a second- to third-grade instructional level, develops rubrics for each of the five reading units she presents. Each rubric depends on her unit plans that indicate what she models and what students practice. Figure 5.7 is the rubric Wanda developed for realistic fiction, and figure 5.8 is her rubric for fantasy.

Repeated skills such as "place/time" are areas where students need more practice. It's easy to see the focus of Wanda's teaching using her anchor text and what students practice using a text from their instructional reading libraries. Students receive the rubric before the unit starts. They paste it in their notebooks, and Wanda reviews each item with them.

Realistic Fiction		Name: _______________	
Skill	**Points**	**Point Break Down**	**Notes**
Figurative Language	/2	+1 example +1 meaning	
Point of View	/2	+1 1st or 3rd person +1 Evidence	
Setting	/2	+1 Place/Time +1 Importance	
Character Trait	/2	+1 Character Development +1 says, thinks, does?	
Conflict/Problem	/1	+1 Conflict/Problem	
Resolution of Conflict	/1	+1 Solution to the conflict	
Conclusion/ Inference	/2	+1 Conclusion/Inference +1 Text evidence	
Total	/12		

FIGURE 5.7. Wanda Waters's rubric for her realistic fiction unit.

Fantasy Unit		Name: _______________	
Skill	**Points**	**Point Break Down**	**Notes**
Problem/Solution	/2	+1 Problem +1 Solution	
Inference/Evidence Complete Sentence	/3	+1 Inference +1 Text Evidence +1 Complete Sentence	
Protagonist	/1	+1 Main Character	
Setting/Impact on Story Complete Sentences	/3	+1 Place/Time +1 How setting affects the story +1 Complete Sentences	
Summary	/3	+1 Beginning +1 Middle +1 End	
Unfamiliar Word/Meaning	/2	+1 Unfamiliar Word +1 Meaning from Text	
Total	/14		

FIGURE 5.8. Wanda Waters's rubric for her fantasy unit.

She says, "It's important for students to know what I'll be looking for when I read notebook entries. It helps them write more detailed and thoughtful entries because they know the expectations."

Notice that Wanda weaves grammar and punctuation into the rubric. "I teach ELL and developing readers," she tells me. "We look at how authors write and why it's important to have complete sentences and varying sentence openings and length. Students always learn in the context of their reading."

In figure 5.9, Wanda's student Audrey evaluates her ability to use context clues to figure out word meanings and why background knowledge about rainforests enabled her to better understand the point of the poem "Rain, She" by David Harrison. A developing reader, Audrey adds a notebook entry that reveals the impact of volume in reading, discussing books, and the models in her teachers' notebook have had on her progress in reading and metacognitive thinking.

Once you've developed reading unit plans (see sample plan and blank form in Appendix E on pages 131–132), developing a rubric is easy. Wanda's students also use the rubric for self-evaluation halfway through the unit and at the end.

Self-Evaluation

Wanda's assessment process starts with her fifth graders self-evaluating their notebook entries. With the rubric as a guide, students use a sticky note to flag pages that reveal their progress. They can write about a flagged page on a sticky note or in their notebooks. Then, students meet one-on-one with Wanda and explain their self-evaluations and answer the questions she poses. Her feedback is positive, and she expresses her concerns by asking questions. Because the school requires that Wanda give letter grades, she invites students to give themselves a grade and explain why that grade is appropriate.

This kind of assessment can develop students' meta-cognition as they think about the quality of their work, point out progress in their own thinking and reasoning, and set one or two goals for areas that need their attention.

Conferring: A Positive Student Experience

Short, frequent conferences with students can increase self-confidence and engagement with reading and writing about reading. Throughout the year, a key part of a conferring should focus on getting to know students so you can better understand how to support them. Start with open-ended questions like:

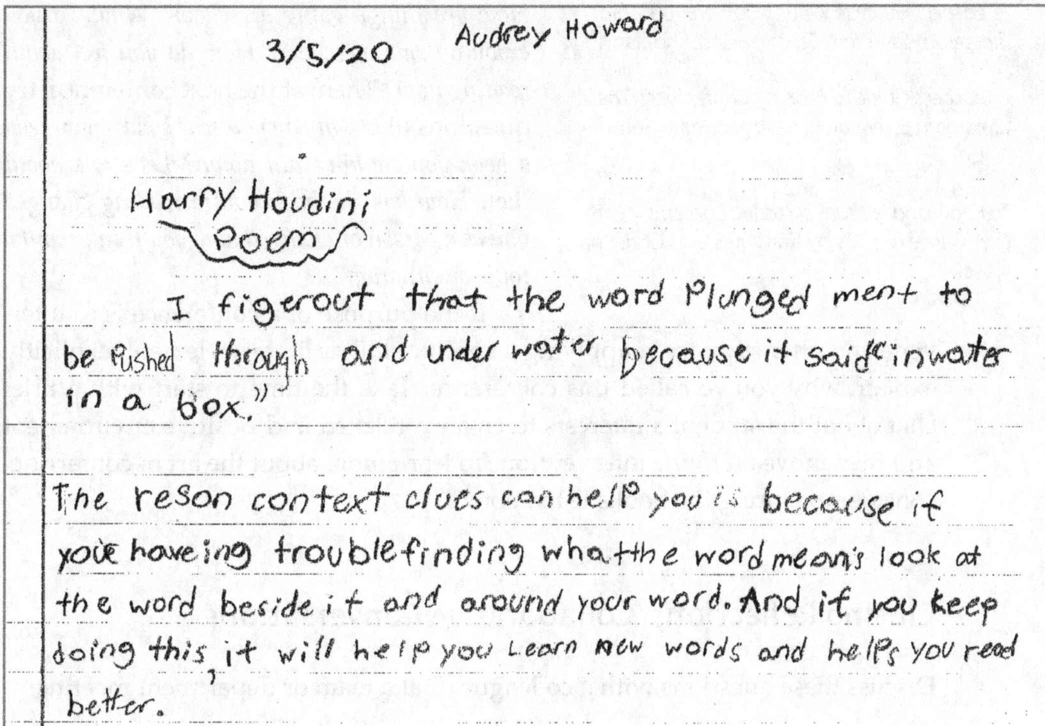

3/5/20 Audrey Howard

Harry Houdini Poem

I figerout that the word Plunged ment to be Pushed through and under water because it said "in water in a box."

The reson context clues can help you is because if you're haveing troublefinding whatthe word mean's look at the word beside it and around your word. And if you keep doing this, it will help you Learn new words and help's you read better.

Rain She

When I watched the video it helped me to know what is happening in the jungles. I learned that People are cutting down trees and animals are loosing their homes.

It helped me better under stand the Poem because the video let's us kno who Rain is and what "she" is and what "she" does. And it help's us know we have to stop people from cutting down trees because thay are takeing homes and oxengen and protection.

FIGURE 5.9. Audrey's notebook entry reveals the progress she is making as her reading volume increases.

A Teacher's Guide to Writing Conferences: The Classroom Essentials Series by Carl Anderson

A Teacher's Guide to Reading Conferences: The Classroom Essentials Series by Jennifer Serravallo

To Know and Nurture a Reader: Conferring with Confidence and Joy by Kari Yates and Christina Nosek

How are things going at school? What do you enjoy outside of school? How do you feel about reading now? Then, at the next conference, try questions like: *Why do you read? Have you read a book you couldn't put down? Let's talk about that. How has the book you're reading changed you as a person or changed how you think about a topic or situation?*

If the purpose of a conference is to intervene and offer support in applying a specific skill or literary element, explicitly explain why you've called this conference. Take the time to start with a brief chat about the student's interests to create a relaxed and positive environment and then move on to the intervention. To learn more about the art of conferring, consider exploring the books listed above.

Closing Reflections: Collaborative Conversations

Discuss these questions with a colleague or at a team or department meeting:

- What are the benefits to students who complete instructional reading at their specific reading levels?
- How does notebook writing support students' comprehension and teachers' understanding of students' needs?
- How are teachers' notebooks powerful teaching tools for students and learning tools for teachers?
- How does the anchor text support your teaching of a reading unit?

6

Core Collections—Core Text and Related Contemporary Texts

I'm meeting with ninth- and tenth-grade teachers at a high school in the Shenandoah Valley to discuss the need for volume in reading. Attending the meeting is the principal and curriculum coordinator, English teachers with classes of students reading three or more years below grade level, and teachers who work with students in regular and honors English classes. The list that follows represents teachers' curricula:

- Read-aloud texts required in regular English classes so students receive the "content." Some teachers ask students to follow along as they read aloud *The Odyssey* by Homer, *Silas Marner* by George Eliot, *Of Mice and Men* by John Steinbeck, and *The Scarlet Letter* by Nathaniel Hawthorne. Students watch Shakespeare's *Romeo and Juliet* and *Julius Caesar* on video.
- Have students read adapted easy versions of classic books such as *The Adventures of Huckleberry Finn* by Mark Twain, *Treasure Island* by Robert Louis Stevenson, *A Tale of Two Cities* by Charles Dickens, etc.
- Read a different district-required classic novel in each one of the first three semesters and a play by William Shakespeare during the fourth semester.

I listen carefully, hoping to find a way to discuss engagement, culturally relevant texts, and volume in reading and then to present alternate ways of organizing instruction around their required core texts. When one teacher expresses her frustration by admitting that her students don't listen and are unengaged when she reads aloud, others agree that they have similar issues. The door opens. I share the research and also recommend teachers set aside fifteen minutes for independent reading each time class meets.

Whether you teach English in middle or high school and have a required curriculum to deliver, the reality you face is that not all students in your class can read and comprehend these texts. Accommodations for students who can't read these texts include the teacher reading the entire book aloud or having students listen to the book on audio. The issue is that students aren't reading.

Some students in your class will be able read the book, yet a group of these students might choose to read CliffsNotes to get the gist of a text that doesn't interest them. Disengaged and lacking the motivation to read, too many students aren't developing reading proficiency or a personal reading life and identity (Goldberg and Houser 2020; Miller and Sharp 2018; Robb and Robb 2020). In addition, the majority of the materials in the canon are white-privileged texts by white authors, resulting in students not reading and discussing books that represent the diversity in our nation and in the world.

Twenty-first century students find relating to the canon a challenge, and they frequently disengage when they feel texts aren't relevant to their lives (Korbey 2019; Styslinger 2017). Equally important, a total of four to six texts a year in regular and honors English classes doesn't offer students the volume in reading they need to improve their skills and reading expertise. This leads to a key question: *If students don't read much, how can they become better at reading?* The answer is easy: *They. Can't.* However, you can increase students' engagement and reading volume by using a core collection that consists of linking a required core text with culturally relevant contemporary texts that have similar themes.

Culturally Relevant Texts, Engagement, Volume, and the Core Collection

The core collection consists of a core book you're required to teach as well as culturally relevant contemporary books related to the core text by themes. Your core required book becomes the common teaching text for your unit of study. Students who can't read it on their own can listen to sections and the rest of the class can read it independently. You can use excerpts from each section that students listen to or read to think aloud and model your emotional and gut reactions and how the book challenges and refines your thinking about hate, love, anxiety, injustice, relationships, etc. The core book as common text also enables you to show students how you infer, identify conflicts and themes, compare and contrast, react to events, and analyze characters. Always keep in mind that the strategy should serve to deepen an understanding of the text—it's the text and not the strategy that's primary. In addition, you can model the kinds of writing students should complete in their notebooks as well as model writing analytical paragraphs and essays that support a position or thesis statement (see Appendix J on developing a thesis and Appendix K on planning and writing an analytical paragraph on pages 141–144).

Using core collections not only increases the amount of reading and discussing students complete, it also supports your students in four ways (Allington and McGill-Franzen 2021; Robb et al. 2023):

1. Since you can select six to ten culturally relevant texts at the diverse reading levels in your classes and have five to seven copies of each text, students have choices of books they can and want to read.
2. Students who choose to read the same related texts can discuss these in small groups.
3. Contemporary, culturally relevant literature offers *all* students' opportunities to learn about diverse cultures.
4. Inclusive texts provide mirrors and windows for students to see themselves in some books and to learn about and develop empathy for others when reading books that don't reflect their own culture or lifestyle (Bishop 1990).

Getting Started

First, you'll need to develop a list of the themes in the core book. Here's the list I brainstormed for *The Pearl* by John Steinbeck, a required text in many ninth-grade classes:

greed	relationships	ignorance
oppression	fear	stereotypes
wealth	status	inequality vs. privilege
poverty	powerless	good vs. evil
superstitions	impact of social structures: family, village, town	

Your librarian can help you find related books; you can also put into any search engine: "Contemporary YA books related to [name of core text]."

Post the list on chart paper and invite students to add themes as they read, discuss, and become aware of them. Next, I brainstorm a list of contemporary inclusive books and narrow the selections down to eight to ten books that meet the range of instructional reading in classes I teach. The books on your list can be the same genre as the core text or may include biography, fantasy, science fiction, historical fiction, informational texts, etc. Once I have the list of ten related contemporary books that students can choose to read, I order five to seven copies of each title to allow for two rounds of selecting related books to read during a semester. If funding is limited, you can check out books from your school's media center and public library. However, books from the public library should remain at school, as you will be responsible for them.

Related Contemporary Texts for the Core Text, *The Pearl*

1. *Lucky Broken Girl* by Ruth Behar (realistic fiction)
2. *Two Roads* by Joseph Bruchac (realistic fiction)
3. *Marcus Vega Doesn't Speak Spanish* by Pablo Cartaya (realistic fiction)
4. *The Red Kayak* by Priscilla Cummings (realistic fiction)
5. *Amal Unbound* by Aisha Saeed (realistic fiction)
6. *The Boy Who Harnessed the Wind* (Young Readers Edition) by William Kamkwamba and Bryan Mealer (memoir)
7. *The Other Wes Moore: One Name, Two Fates* by Wes Moore (memoir)
8. *All American Boys* by Jason Reynolds and Brendan Kiely (realistic fiction).
9. *They Called Us Enemy* by George Takei (graphic memoir)
10. *Enrique's Journey: The True Story of a Boy Determined to Reunite with His Mother* (YA adaptation) by Sonia Nazario (informational text)

You don't have to read all of the related books; if you can, however, it makes listening to students' thinking, their generating ideas, and their discussions of related themes a richer experience for you. Listen to their discussions and ask questions to provoke deeper thinking, but avoid any temptation to control the direction students are taking as long as it relates their book to a theme or themes in the core text. Remember, this is an opportunity for student-led literary conversations, and they will need time and space to analyze the book and make thematic connections to *The Pearl*.

Organize Your Core Text

I divide *The Pearl*, a short novel, into three chunks or sections, each between twenty-two and forty pages long, and then I decide how much to cover in a week. Note that each chunk ends with a chapter closing.

First chunk: End of chapter three

Second chunk: End of chapter five

Third chunk: End of chapter six

After students complete their reading or listening to a chunk, I present one to three mini-lessons, repeating it for those students who need to listen and observe again. The number of times you think-aloud and model for students depends on their needs as readers and critical thinkers. Mini-lesson content can include reflecting on themes, analyzing dialogue and characters' actions, or applying a reading strategy. Keep in mind that students' responses to mini-lessons and their questions can and should change as you respond to the needs they reveal. Sometimes, you'll repeat a mini-lesson to a small group while others read or complete notebook writing. What follows are the mini-lessons I plan to present for each chunk of text in *The Pearl*. These can change because they should respond to students' needs.

Mini-lessons for First Chunk

- Review symbolism: songs, pearl, scorpion
- Fear as a driving force
- Inequality vs. privilege

Mini-lessons for Second Chunk

- Inferring
- Quotes from text and connections to themes
- Greed and privilege

Mini-lessons for Third Chunk

- The evolving metaphor of music and songs
- Gender issues
- Symbolism and symbolic gestures

The Core Text: Your Common Teaching Text

Using your core text, you can model how to think about and analyze the book as well as set the stage for discussing related books by providing students with a mental model of what taking deep dives into texts look like. Always move from thinking aloud to involving students so they practice while you're there to support them.

- Read and discuss the core text in chunks of three to four chapters. Students can discuss with the same partner throughout the book or by simply turning and talking.
- Explain how the book affects your feelings toward characters and events.
- Discuss why the book has adjusted or changed your thinking about people, events, themes, and life.
- Use literary elements to engage students by discussing protagonist and problems; antagonists and how each works against the protagonist; minor characters and how they affect the protagonist and plot; settings; conflicts; points of view; symbolism; and themes.
- Identify the personality traits of the protagonist and support this with text evidence.
- Show how other characters and events change one or two of the protagonist's personality traits, beliefs, or values.

Your modeling, think-alouds, and discussions with students can generate ideas for students to write about reading in their notebooks. Use your teachers' notebook to show students what a response looks like.

Teachers' Notebooks: Sample Models for Writing about Reading

Emotional reactions are often readers' first responses to books, and these can bond them to characters, people, events, conflicts, and decisions. Two responses that can capture students' initial gut reactions to a text's contents are "four words" and "emotions raised."

Four Words: Model in a "cold write" four words that came to mind after reading or hearing a section—words you associated with the text. Head a page in your teachers' notebook and write the four words. Next, choose one and link it to the text with details from that section.

Example from the First Chunk of *The Pearl*

Four words: deceitful, greedy, cunning, and selfish

Connect one word to the story: The deceitful doctor who refused to help Coyotito after a scorpion bit the infant returns to Kino's hut when he hears about the pearl. He treats the baby and then asks when Kino will pay his bill. The doctor pays the family a visit only because he can now extract money from them. He plays on their ignorance, makes the baby vomit, and deceives both parents into thinking he's cured Coyotito.

Example from the Third Chunk of *The Pearl*

Four words: fear, relief, sadness, obsessive

Connect one word to the story: Relief washes over me when Kino, with Juana at his side, throws the pearl into the ocean. The last reflections Kino sees in the pearl are the dead Coyotito and evil faces. He now accepts that the pearl is ugly, misshapen, and evil, and the music it generates is "distorted and insane." Throwing the pearl back into the sea is symbolic of Kino ridding himself and Juana of the evil and destruction that an obsession for wealth has brought to their lives.

To the teacher: Now show and share with students the emotions a section of text raised within you, choose one, and in a cold write, link the emotion to the text.

You can also model notebook writing about literary elements (see Appendix D on pages 128–130), conflicts, themes, characters' personality traits, changes in characters and the cause of these changes, inferring, comparison and contrast, decisions, etc. Ask students to move beyond memorizing definitions of literary terms and find specific examples of terms in *The Pearl* (or any other text). In addition, take time to show students how you write about the changes in thinking about themes, people, and life that the core text caused.

When you're halfway through the core text, you can share related texts with students. Briefly introduce each text with a book talk. Read part of the first chapter or the promotional writing on the back cover or the inside flap. If you've read the book, explain why it's a compelling read. Organize books by readability and direct groups to specific sets of books. If a student wants to read a book outside of those you suggest, listen to that student's reasons. If they have the background knowledge or are passionate about the topic, genre, or author, let them try. Privately, explain that they might have to reread parts and that you will be available for support.

> Check in with students who've chosen a book above their instructional reading level after they complete the first chunk and ask them to tell you about the book. If they can't tell you much, invite them to reread the first chapter and then tell you what they recall. If recall is detailed, explain that rereading is important for them to recall those specifics. If recall remains sketchy, explain that it's best to save the book for a later round of related texts and choose another book and group. Taking the time to check after the students complete the first chunk is the ideal time to make adjustments, as catching up with the reading in a different book is still doable.

Students Select Their First Book Related to the Core Text

Set aside time for students to browse through texts, though bear in mind that the number of books per title limits the number of students in a group. If the study spans an entire semester, students can read and discuss two to three related texts. Encourage all students to read extra books that interest them and are related to the themes in the core text (Afflerbach 2022; Dorn and Soffos 2005; Urbanksi 2015; Vaughn and Massey 2021). You can generate excitement for related texts and maintain a focus on the process when you:

- Display the related texts at diverse instructional reading levels.
- Give students choices when they select books.
- Have students divide related texts into three to five chunks, depending on the book's length. End each chunk before a new chapter begins.
- Have students place sticky notes at the end of each chunk. On the sticky note, students write: "Stop to Think."
- Negotiate a deadline date for each chunk with students.
- Have students read their related books at school if your literacy block has enough time. Otherwise, they can read at home. However, this opens the possibility of students forgetting to bring the related book to class after completing each chunk. To prevent this, note on the chalkboard reminders of the dates books need to come to school and periodically call students' attention to those dates.

Gently monitor students as they select related books and make sure they can read and comprehend their text choices.

Open-Ended Prompts for Discussing Related Books

Besides discussing themes that connect to the core text—in this case, *The Pearl* by John Steinbeck—here are some suggestions for discussing related books. Invite groups to select two to four prompts that apply to their related text and discuss each one supporting their thinking with text evidence.

- Evaluate how a character responds to a specific situation. Describe the situation and the character's reaction. How did this change your feelings and/or thoughts about the character?
- Find one event or person that created significant change in the protagonist's or another character's life. Name the event and explain the changes and how they affect the character and his or her community.
- Predict what you think will happen next and give evidence from the book that supports your prediction.
- Identify a problem and explain how the character solved it. Would you have solved it differently? Explain how.

- Identify a decision a character made and evaluate whether it was a good or poor decision. Use text evidence to support your position. Explain what you would have done in the same situation.
- Choose two antagonistic forces and show how each one worked against the protagonist. Show how one or both of these antagonistic forces changed the character.
- Describe how another character or event changed the main character and explain the change you observed.
- Identify two characters who like each other and have a good relationship or two who don't get along. Use text evidence to explain the causes for the positive or negative relationship. What did you learn about relationships?
- List four to five significant events in the book in sequence or the order in which they happened. Explain why each event was significant. To do this, you can link the event to a character's decision, a problem, a conflict, a solution to a problem, or a setting.
- Choose a setting you consider important. Use text details to explain why it was important to the protagonist, antagonist(s), a problem, a decision, or a conflict.
- Identify two big problems the protagonist solved. For each one, explain the actions the protagonist took and the outcome. Evaluate the character's actions.
- How are you and the protagonist alike? Different?
- Compare and contrast a theme or the protagonist in your related book to a similar one in the core book.
- Choose and write in your notebook a quote that spoke to you. Explain why it's important to the story and to one or more themes.

Suggestions for Students' Notebook Writing

Students can write about a prompt they selected and discussed with a partner or group. In addition to the questions/prompts that follow, ask students what they would like to write about. Tapping into students' ideas can let you know what students found important and compelling about the reading (Crowder 2020; Robb and Robb 2020; Robb et al. 2023). Moreover, it offers them choice!

- Invite students to select a question/prompt they discussed and complete a journal entry about it based on your model.

- Ask students to connect a theme, problem, or conflict in their related book to one that was similar to one in the core book. Then, ask students to explain and show similarities.
- Invite students to choose one or two of the questions/prompts that follow for notebook writing. Remind them to jot notes before writing.
- How did this book make you feel? Identify two emotions and explain what in the story caused them. Did you experience similar emotions with the core book? Explain.
- Did you relate to or connect with a character? Explain why. Was the character similar to or different from a character in the core book?
- What do you have in common with the protagonist? Problems? Relationships? Conflicts? Be specific and explain using details from the core and/or related texts.
- Did the characters in the core book have problems that were similar to those in your related book? Explain.
- Explain three things you learned about a character's or person's culture that you didn't know before reading the book.

Students' notebook writing reflects their depth of thinking as they explore contemporary literature, discuss it in a small group, and then write reflections in their notebooks. Figure 6.1 shows the connections a ninth grader, Jaime, makes between *The Pearl* and *All American Boys*. Notice how thinking about an event in both texts enables Jaime to explain the effects the event had on the protagonist, their families, and others in their communities (Anderson et al. 2021; Burke 2012).

Possible Assessments

In addition to assessing students' work by conferring, reading students' notebook writing, and asking them to self-evaluate their progress, you can invite students to suggest other assessments (Crowder 2020; Heritage 2021. Students I've worked with have created a website for the core book and related books they've read, developed and conducted surveys about stereotyping people and defending human rights, composed and illustrated a series of poems based on their reading, and video-recorded peers and adults answering questions students developed.

A Life-Changing Event

In both *The Pearl* by John Steinbeck and *All American Boys* by Jason Reynolds, one event changes the course of the protagonists' lives. On the last page of *The Pearl*, Steinbeck shows how Kino now views the pearl before he throws it back into the ocean. Instead of smooth and beautiful and worth much money, the pearl's surface is now "gray and ulcerous." Instead of hope for educating his son and living a better life with his wife Juana and having the priest marry them, the event of finding the pearl has brought pain and evil into Kino's life: the death of his baby son Coyotito, the burning of his house, running from thieves, and committing murder to save the pearl for himself brings grief, pain, and evil to Kino and his family. When Kino throws the pearl back into the ocean, he lets go of the evil that has controlled his life; the action symbolizes a new start, a new beginning for Kino and Juana together.

As in *The Pearl*, one event changes the course of Rashad's life in *All American Boys* by Jason Reynolds. The event occurs in a convenience store where Rashad is buying snacks. Rashad bends to get his wallet from his bag when the lady behind him crashes into Rashad and drops a bottle of beer she was holding. Before Katie can explain, a cop and a store clerk accuse Rashad of trying to steal a bag of chips. When Rashad denies stealing and tries to explain, the cop slams Rashad to the ground, accuses him of trying to resist arrest, and cuffs Rashad and delivers several blows. Now Rashad is in the hospital with a broken nose and internal bleeding and will have to appear in court. In the hospital, Rashad's life is changing, and he has to process some heavy stuff. His dad, a former police officer, shot an unarmed black kid whom he believed was reaching for a weapon. The shot paralyzed the young man, who was innocent, and Rashad's dad resigns. At this point, Rashad sees his father as flawed, and Rashad needs to process this information. Once released from the hospital, Rashad finds out that his peers at school and his teachers have planned a protest and that this hashtag is all over the Internet: #RashadIsAbsentAgainToday. The protest is a *die-in* and Berry, Rashad's brother's activist girlfriend, reads, through a megaphone, a list of names of unarmed black men and women killed by the police. Rashad joins the protest and removes his face bandages so everyone can see his injuries. His father comes to the protest and this shows a change in his son. Quinn, a white kid who saw the cop beating up Rashad, after a lot of soul-searching gives a statement to the police. Rashad has survived and the crowd of young and old, white and black protesters offers hope for change in the future. This event changed Rashad's life as he became a symbol of the need for changing white policemen abusing black men and women. The event also changed Rashad's relationships with his dad and showed that witnesses to the unwarranted beating of Rashad were willing to come forward to testify.

One event in *The Pearl* and one event in *All American Boys* changed the lives of Kino and Rashad. But each event also changed others in their family and how their communities viewed them.

FIGURE 6.1. Connecting a contemporary text to the core text.

Conferring to Assess

Schedule short conferences with each student and discuss the related and core books. Jot notes and keep dated records of your student-teacher conferences. Here are possible questions to ask:

- How did you feel when the book ended? Explain why.
- What part did you enjoy most or affected you deeply? Explain why.
- Did this book change your thinking about an issue? Explain in what way.
- What did you learn about the protagonist and his or her family and/or friends?
- How is the protagonist's life different from yours? The same as yours? Give specific examples.
- What emotions did the book raise within you? How did these emotions affect your understandings of character, plot, decisions, or themes?
- What did you learn about yourself as a reader from this book?

Notebook Writing as an Assessment

- Ask students to place a sticky note on a notebook entry they want you to read. Then, choose an entry at random and read it. Note your reactions and questions on a sticky note; don't write in the students' notebook.
- Read both, and on a sticky note, jot the strengths and progress you observed. Then, set priorities and ask students one or two questions about areas they need to reflect on and refine.
- Invite students to set a goal in their notebooks for new entries.

Students' Self-Evaluations Are Assessments

Have students review several of their own notebook entries and respond to these questions or queries they create in their notebooks (Crowder 2020; Gonzales 2014). Students' self-evaluations can be written or presented during a conference with the teacher taking notes on what the students say. Take a few minutes to review your notes with students and compare their observations with yours.

- Are my entries more detailed? Give an example.
- Do I include text evidence to support my thoughts? Give an example.
- Do I jot notes before writing? Why does this help?
- Am I writing more to show my thinking? Give an example.
- Are the books I'm reading changing my thinking? Explain how.
- Have my literary tastes changed during this time? Discuss what you were reading before and what you're reading now.

Notice the honesty in the example Helena, an eighth grader, provides in her digital notebook. She also shows that students require time to embrace notebook writing and experience its benefits in order to develop a deeper understanding of a text.

> *The first two weeks I wrote very little. I thought this (notebook writing) was a waste of time. The entry that shows a change in my feelings about notebook writing was when you asked us to write our feelings about sit-ins during the Jim Crow era. That was a great read-aloud (*Freedom on the Menu *by Carole Boston Weatherford). It woke me up to how privileged I am and the depth of rejection and inequality African Americans endured then and I think still endure now. In that entry, I gave evidence and wrote a full page. That entry marks the change in my notebook writing.*

If you agree with a student's self-evaluation, share that during a conference. When your thoughts differ from the students, discuss them and invite the student to comment. I'm delighted when students change my point of view, as it illustrates how attuned to their process they are.

Assess with a Single-Point Rubric

Besides creating a traditional rubric, consider moving to a single-point rubric (Gonzales 2014). When you develop a single-point rubric that breaks a writing task into categories, students know your expectations for a specific task. The single-point rubric is more open-ended than the rubric that assigns points to specific skills. Moreover, using this type of rubric takes students' focus off of grades by not creating numbered boundaries found in traditional rubrics. Because single-point rubrics are more open-ended and can be created by the students themselves, their creativity and critical thinking develop as they craft a piece that fulfills the assignment. It also encourages teacher feedback that can enable the students to revise their writing in addressing specific suggestions. You can use this type of rubric to evaluate students' notebook writing as well as analytical paragraphs and essays. Figure 6.2 is an example of a single-point rubric for an analytical essay.

Things to improve	How I will assess your essay	Things that were beyond basic expectations
	Thesis or Position Statement: States position clearly and accurately	
	Supporting Evidence: Selects enough powerful evidence to support the thesis/position	
	Transitions: Smooth from paragraph to paragraph	
	Conclusion: Not only wraps up your position but leaves something more for reader to think about that emerges from the topic	
	Length of Essay: Write as much as you need to prove your thesis—try to keep the essay to two to three one-and-one-half-spaced typed pages	
	Grammar & usage: I'll be looking for paragraphing, varying sentence openings, and sentence structure	

FIGURE 6.2. Sample Single-Point Rubric.

Note that the single-point rubric offers guidance but far less direction from teachers, leaving room for students to approach the writing from their own unique point of view. This type of rubric also provides space for feedback from the teacher, a peer, or a self-evaluation by the student.

You can use the core collection unit for *The Pearl* to inform your planning of similar units and make adjustments that respond to your students' needs.

Use Inquiry and Collaboration to Plan a Core Collection Unit

When planning units with core and culturally relevant contemporary books, it's beneficial to pose questions and work with colleagues as you search for related books and generate themes for the core text (Daniels 2017; MacKenzie 2016).

- What are the themes of your core book?
- How will you find related culturally relevant texts that reflect "mirrors, windows, and sliding glass doors?" (Bishop 1990)
- How many weeks will the unit take?

- What will you use as a read-aloud text or texts?
- Can you compose open-ended questions to ask students to discuss using their related books? (An open-ended question has at least two answers that the text/illustrations can support. See page 58.)
- How many related books will each student read?
- What kinds of notebook writing will you model and have students try?
- How can you and your colleagues support one another through a unit?

As you select books, make sure they represent the range of reading levels in your classes, so students can choose books they can read, learn from, and enjoy.

Two Sample Core and Related Text Units for Middle School

Middle school curriculum varies greatly from one required novel a semester for students, which doesn't provide enough reading volume, to a workshop model in which students select instructional reading books and read several during a semester (see chapter five). Note that both units include books representing the diverse cultures in our nation.

Middle School Core Text: *Anne Frank: The Diary of a Young Girl*, Anne Frank

Themes: fear, separation, destruction, loss, friendship, hopes and dreams, genocide, prejudice, hatred, isolation, death

1. *They Called Us Enemy* by George Takei (memoir)
2. *The Beloved World of Sonia Sotomayor* by Sonia Sotomayor (memoir)
3. *Invasion* by Walter Dean Myers (historical fiction)
4. *Into the Fire* by Dakota Meyer (memoir)
5. *Inside Out and Back Again* by Thanhhà Lai (verse novel)
6. *Chinese Cinderella: The True Story of an Unwanted Daughter* by Adeline Yen Mah (memoir)
7. *Before We Were Free* by Julia Alvarez (diary)
8. *Greta Thunberg: No One Is Too Small to Make a Difference* by Greta Thunberg (speeches)
9. *I Am Malala: How One Girl Stood Up for Education and Was Shot* by Malala Yousafzai (memoir)
10. *Brown Girl Dreaming* by Jacqueline Woodson (verse novel)

Middle School Core Text: *The Call of the Wild* by Jack London

Themes: perseverance, knowledge, wisdom, primitive life, suffering, loyalty, pride, man and nature, respect, civilization vs. the wildness of the natural world, extremes, relationships, power of love, violence

1. *Shipwreck at the Bottom of the World: The Extraordinary Story of Shackleton and the Endurance* by Jennifer Armstrong (informational text)
2. *The Cay* by Theodore Taylor (adventure fiction)
3. *Hatchet* by Gary Paulsen (realistic fiction)
4. *Brown Girl Dreaming* by Jacqueline Woodson (memoir)
5. *The Last Panther* by Todd Mitchell (realistic fiction)
6. *The Heart of the Sea: The Tragedy of the Whaleship* Essex (Young Readers Edition) by Nathaniel Philbrick (informational text)
7. *Copper Sun* by Sharon Draper (realistic fiction)
8. *The Age of Miracles* by Karen Thompson Walker (realistic fiction)
9. *Amal Unbound* by Aisha Saeed (realistic fiction)
10. *Into the Wild* by Jon Krakauer (informational text)

Three Sample Core and Related Text Units for High School

High school English curricula usually have a set of required texts for each grade level that can vary for AP, honors, and regular English classes. The sample core collection units that follow pair a required text with contemporary culturally relevant literature and transform a white-privileged curriculum into one that represents the cultural diversity in our country. As students increase their engagement through choice, they will read about people and issues relevant to their lives and connect these to the core book.

High School Core Text: *Romeo and Juliet* by William Shakespeare

Themes: gangs, young first love, rebellion, relationships, intense power of love, family, friends, violence, death, fate, the gulf between youth and adults

1. *Romiette and Julio* by Sharon Draper (Realistic fiction)
2. *I Am Not Your Perfect Mexican Daughter* by Erika L. Sanchez (realistic fiction)
3. *The Other Wes Moore: One Name, Two Fates* by Wes Moore (memoir)
4. *West Side Story* by Arthur Laurents (play)
5. *Becoming Beatriz* by Tami Charles (realistic fiction)

6. *The Fault in Our Stars* by John Green (realistic fiction).
7. *Written in the Stars* by Aisha Saeed (realistic fiction)
8. *Harbor Me* by Jacqueline Woodson (memoir)
9. *Love, Hate & Other Filters* by Samira Ahmed (realistic fiction)
10. *Internment* by Samira Ahmed (realistic fiction)

High School Core Text: *The Scarlet Letter* by Nathaniel Hawthorne
Themes: adultery, revenge, compassion, forgiveness, guilt and blame, justice, injustice, judgment, isolation

1. *Man's Search for Meaning* (Young Adult Edition) by Victor E. Frankl (informational text)
2. *The Kite Runner* by Khaled Hosseini (realistic fiction)
3. *They Called Us Enemy* by George Takei, Justin Eisinger, Steven Scott, and Harmony Becker (graphic memoir)
4. *Salt to the Sea* by Ruta Sepetys (historical fiction)
5. *Amal Unbound* by Aisha Saeed (realistic fiction)
6. *Written in the Stars* by Aisha Saeed (realistic fiction)
7. *Lovely War* by Julie Berry (historical fiction)
8. *The Night Diary* by Veera Hiranandani (fictional letters)
9. *The Age of Miracles* by Karen Thompson Walker (speculative fiction)
10. *The Outcast: A Modern Retelling of* The Scarlet Letter by Jolina Petersheim (realistic fiction).

High School Core Text: *1984* by George Orwell
Themes: control, loss of freedom, propaganda, love, loyalty, betrayal, psychological manipulation, technology, information control, brainwashing

1. *Song Below Water* by Bethany Morrow (fantasy)
2. *Tankborn* by Karen Sandler (science fiction)
3. *Matched* by Ally Condie (dystopian fiction)
4. *The City of Ember* by Jeanne DuPrau (dystopian fiction)
5. *Red Rising* by Pierce Brown (science fiction)
6. *Your Robot Dog Will Die* by Arin Greenwood (speculative fiction)
7. *Unearthly Things* by Michelle Gagnon (thriller)

8. *Legend* by Marie Lu (science fiction)
9. *MEM* by Bethany Morrow (science fiction)
10. *Trazer: Kids of Stolen Tomorrow* by Joseph O Adegboyega-Edun (dystopian fiction)
11. *A Blade So Black (The Nightmare–Verse, 1)* by L. L. McKinney (urban fantasy)

Core Collections Push Students' Thinking

By comparing and contrasting core and related texts, students can observe how contemporary authors use plot and characters to shape themes in contexts that make their books relevant to students' lives today. Yet, there's more you can ask students to explore, reflect upon, and think about besides reading, discussing, and writing. You can provide opportunities for them to move beyond traditional learning in English classes to developing a global perspective by reading the world (Afflerbach 2022; Dorn and Soffos 2005; Hinchman and Sheridan-Thomas 2022).

Ask Students to Read the World

When students' reading, discussions, and investigations move from one text to a diversity of texts, they have opportunities to "read" a part of the world and broaden their knowledge of a topic. Reading the world can include exploring blogs, photographs, videos, and oral texts such as interviews and conversations. As students widen their "reading," they can explore culturally diverse perspectives and absorb information from oral, visual, and written texts.

Inviting groups of students to use inquiry to extend their reading of core texts enables them to come to see books as one of many ways to learn and read the world. The "what" and "where" questions can lead to exploring ideas beyond those presented in the core and related texts. Questions such as: What else do I want to know about genocide *(Anne Frank: The Diary of a Young Girl)*? What else can I learn about survival in harsh and extreme environments *(The Call of the Wild)*? What else can I explore and understand about gang mentalities and parental restrictions *(Romeo and Juliet)*?

Wondering where to find resources in addition to books? Invite students to interview people at school or in their community, read blogs, watch videos by experts, or study photographs and displays online from museums around the world. The platforms are only limited by students' and teachers' imaginations.

And this brings me to considering a larger purpose for the question, *Why read?* The answer means much more than to amass information or to pass a test. In their book, *Comprehension: The Skill, Will, and Thrill of Reading* (2020), Douglas Fisher and Nancy Frey paraphrase what P. David Pearson said about reading and comprehension at his retirement party (see pages 10–11). Pearson puts comprehension as the primary goal of reading and explains it as part of the process of learning to read when he says that ". . . comprehension may be important if it is on the pathway to critical reasoning and problem solving, which may be important if it is the pathway to action in the world. Changing something that matters."

If one accepts Pearson's thinking, which I do, then traditional views of comprehension such as answering a set of questions or completing worksheets to show recall are hardly enough—they're even inconsequential. When teachers and students understand that to read is to change one's thinking, then analytical thinking and generating ideas on how to make the world a better place are important results. So, learning about Anne Frank and genocide is only a first step. The next steps can include speaking out for human rights by writing to local and state politicians with suggestions for positive changes. Pearson asks so much more of students than many schools do today.

Using inquiry to ask "what" and "where" questions can move students beyond thinking the facts are enough. They aren't. The facts need to be reflected upon, analyzed, and viewed through the lens of using what we've learned to make the world a better place—as Pearson put it, "to change something that matters!" Moving from reading books to reading the world ensures that we teachers nurture critical and creative thinkers capable of solving problems that affect everyone on our planet.

Closing Reflections: Collaborative Conversations

- What are the benefits of including culturally relevant contemporary literature alongside the study of a required core text?
- Why do you agree or disagree with Pearson's definition of comprehension?
- How do core collections deepen students' understanding of themselves and of diverse cultures and lifestyles? Why is this important?
- Why is it important to have students "read the world?"

7 Suggestions for Getting Started and Moving Forward

In "Intervention All Day Long: New Hope for Struggling Readers," Richard Allington writes:

> We need to reconceptualize intervention for struggling readers as something that must occur all day long. Intervention cannot just consist of those few minutes working with a reading specialist. Let's face the fact that too often, the texts in students' hands are appropriate for the highest achieving half of students, ensuring that the rich get richer because only the best readers have books in their hands that they can read fluently, and with understanding. *All* students need texts of an appropriate level of complexity *all day long* to thrive in school. (13)

Allington argues for volume in reading, as his research reveals that for all students to learn and improve every day in every subject, they need easy access to books and materials they can read and understand. However, with one text for all students, a large number of learners travel through the school day unable to read required materials, and as their reading volume diminishes, so does their interest, comprehension, and critical thinking. By having culturally relevant texts at varied reading levels, you can reverse this trend and increase students' volume in reading.

However, getting started and moving forward with teaching for volume in reading for ELA and content, teachers can find overwhelming. When you and your colleagues work as a team with school leaders to identify needs, to find funding for books and reading materials, and to create a plan to gradually reach specific goals, you'll have the support to create positive change. What follows are suggestions to discuss with colleagues and school administrators for getting started and developing reasonable goals.

For ELA Teachers: Start with Independent Reading

Once you accept the premise that building classroom libraries and integrating culturally relevant texts into your curriculum can make a huge difference in students' desire to read for pleasure and to learn, then change will rise to the top of your to-do list. Taking that first step makes the next steps easier, especially when you work with like-minded colleagues. Start with independent reading because, with choice and time to read at school, it's one of the best ways to develop your students' reading identities and desire to read (Krashen, 2004; Miller and Sharp, 2018; Ness et al., Robb & Robb, 2018; Robb and Robb, 2020).

Review chapter one for information on volume in reading and check out chapter three on independent reading. If you have a rich independent reading curriculum, then introduce the anchor text, your common text, and teaching tools when students read different books (see pages 79–83.

Study your schedule and decide whether you can include independent reading every day or at least two to three times a week. Consider discussing with your principal finding ways to add more time for independent reading. For example, middle school principal Evan Robb takes a few minutes off each block to create a twenty-minute daily class for independent reading and intervention.

Assess your classroom library and decide whether you need to add culturally relevant texts and more books at a range of reading levels and in different genres to increase choices for your students. Meet with your principal to discuss the possibility of annual funding for classroom libraries, so your collection remains relevant to students, and missing books can be replaced.

Model how to choose "good fit" books and explain why independent reading can improve students' reading skills and develop a desire to read.

Set a reasonable timeline for starting a classroom library or enlarging your present library. Consider adding ebook platforms that support virtual and in-person learning.

Keep track of students' independent reading by taping a reading log form (see Appendix I on page 140) at the back of their notebooks. Set aside time for them to log completed or abandoned books. Use these logs to assess students' reading volume, the variety of genres they are reading, and to discuss specific books during reading conferences.

Use authentic assessments such as monthly book talks and writing book reviews to post on your class website and/or the school's website.

Moving Forward: Add One Instructional Reading Unit

Once independent reading of self-selected books is flourishing in your class, it's time to look at instructional reading and formative assessments that permit you to monitor students' progress through daily observations, brief scheduled conferences, and reading a few pages from their notebooks.

Review appendix pages 125–144 so you're familiar with their contents.

Develop one new instructional reading unit so students have additional choices and can read accessible texts. Review chapters five and six and decide whether you'll try instructional reading unit libraries or the core collection by adding books related to the core text. Work with your librarian to determine the availability of books that meet the range of instructional reading levels in your classes. Add additional units only when you're comfortable with the one(s) you've developed.

Practice planning and then teaching with an anchor text—your common text that allows you to model your emotional reactions, as well as how you think about reading, writing about reading, and building vocabulary with an anchor chart (see pages 79–83 for a review of teaching with an anchor text).

Observe students during your anchor text lessons, independent reading, instructional reading, and writing about reading in notebooks while making the rounds by circulating among students and during scheduled conferences. These observations will enable you to decide who needs support and/or interventions and who can work with a partner or independently.

Confer with students to celebrate progress, learn about their reading identities and attitudes, provide support, and discuss how a book they enjoyed affected their feelings and thinking about the characters and people as well as themes such as justice/injustice, obstacles, relationships, etc.

Model with your teachers' notebook and "cold write" under a document camera to show how you plan and compose a response. Your notebook is a resource that students can reread to refresh their memories before writing their own notebook responses (see pages 87–88 for information on teachers' notebooks).

Organize a book room to store multiple texts for instructional reading units and sets of books for book clubs. If your school doesn't have a small room, work with members of your team or department to decide which sets each one of you will store in your classrooms.

Use students' notebook entries to learn about their comprehension of instructional reading (see pages 88–93 for more on readers' notebooks).

Continue Moving Forward

Changing instruction can be frustrating and stressful. When you collaborate with one or a few colleagues who have similar goals, you create a support network that can encourage you to try new teaching strategies while diminishing the frustration and anxiety that often accompany taking risks. Give yourself the gift of time and continue to move forward only when you're comfortable adding a new instructional element.

Add more reading units when you feel ready. Trying one unit, reflecting on it, and having conversations with colleagues that are also trying a differentiated unit can help you clarify questions and concerns and raise your comfort level to a point where you are ready to introduce a second unit.

Introduce book clubs and establish with students a reading schedule that includes time to stop and discuss a chunk of text (see pages 57–58 to review book clubs).

Organize groups of students to provide support, to introduce student-led literary conversations, and/or for enrichment such as creating and performing readers' theater scripts (review suggestions in chapter four).

Introduce students to self-evaluation with a single-point rubric and have individuals develop their own criteria for writing or a project and then self-evaluate (see pages 111–112 to review single-point rubrics).

In addition to teaching reading and writing, you might also be teaching social studies, math, or science. Since research shows that students benefit from reading throughout the school day, you'll want to bring volume in reading to content subjects by finding alternate texts on a topic at instructional reading levels that meet the needs of the students you teach. Share this information with other content teachers.

Bring Reading Volume to Content Subjects: The Role of Disciplinary Literacy

Disciplinary literacy emphasizes the tools unique to a discipline—tools content teachers and experts use to engage in the work of that discipline (Lent 2015). When textbooks are the main resource students have, their learning in content subjects can be limited. What follows are content subjects and the kinds of reading teachers might include.

History: Students need to learn how to read primary documents, essays, blogs, and informational books written by historians.

Math: Teachers need to show students how to read and unpack the language of math problems and figure out ways to solve them. They can read books about famous mathematicians and watch videos such as those from the Khan Academy that support understanding challenging concepts.

Science: Students should read essays and journal articles by scientists, excerpts from scientists' journals, blogs, books, lab reports, and informational texts.

By using a variety of reading materials, content teachers can find accessible texts to acquire information for the range of reading levels in their classrooms. The need to read to gain background knowledge and vocabulary as well as to learn a range of perspectives on a topic or theory is key to the content learning middle and high school students do. So is having access to books that are "mirrors, windows, and sliding glass doors" in those classes (Bishop 1990).

Getting Started for Content Teachers: Develop Classroom Libraries

Science, social studies, and math teachers can provide access to outstanding books in their subjects by having classroom libraries filled with biographies, picture books, historical fiction, poetry, informational texts, and magazines on a variety of reading levels. How much richer and broader students' learning will be if they read culturally diverse materials related to specific content areas in addition to reading textbooks. Having a collection of books and other reading materials in each content class offers students reading choices across a range of readability levels.

Suggestions for Using Content Subject Libraries

Inviting students to use content classroom libraries allows them to deepen their knowledge and understanding of topics within a specific subject, giving them a broader view of the subject and at the same time contributing to their overall volume in reading and reading the world. It's possible to find time without diminishing the amount of curriculum you're required to teach. Here are a few suggestions to consider:

Ask students to select a book and read it. Then, set aside one class, organize students into small groups, and have them share some key points they learned from their book with each other. Students can discuss: *Why did I choose this book?*

How did the book expand my thinking or knowledge of a topic? How did the book increase my interest in the topic? What about the topic did I find fascinating?

A book talk each semester. Ask students to select a book they completed and prepare a book talk (see pages 57–58 for guidelines).

Integrate library books into a unit study. Offer books from your classroom library and school media center that enhance a topic students are studying. Invite students to choose and read a book and then hold small-group discussions using questions like: *How does the information in my book relate to our topic? What did I learn about the topic that's new information? Did the book change my thinking about the topic? Explain how. What are a few questions the book raised, and how can I explore some answers? Are there videos on this topic I could watch, learn from, and share?*

As you integrate books from your classroom library into your curriculum, invite students to suggest ways they'd enjoy connecting them to their learning. Having outstanding books at students' fingertips can spark their interest in topics because books include stories that help students learn and understand information (Wells 1985).

Closing Thoughts

Every student in your class deserves to improve their reading expertise and develop a personal reading life. This will most likely occur when you increase students' volume in reading, discussions about books, and writing about reading in notebooks. In addition, and during frequent conferences, encourage reflection on their reading progress and how books have changed their thinking. With your support and understanding of students' needs, reading can become a positive, lifelong experience that enables students to be analytical, think critically, problem solve, and best of all, read to learn and for pleasure!

Appendix A

Interest Inventory

Directions: Complete the inventory on a separate piece of paper. You can respond in sentences or bulleted lists.

- What is your favorite subject or activity at school? Explain why.
- What are two or three things you enjoy doing most in your free time at home?
- What subject at school do you find most challenging? Explain why.
- What are your favorite sports to watch?
- What are your favorite sports to play?
- Do you dance, play an instrument, sing in a choir, or act in plays? Explain why this experience is important to you.
- What are your favorite video games?
- What kinds of music do you listen to? Do you have a favorite band or soloist?
- If you could learn anything, what would you want to learn? Explain why this interests you.
- What kinds of books do you enjoy the most when you reading on your own? Name a book you found memorable.
- What clubs, groups, teams, and organizations do you belong to at school and outside of school?
- What are you usually doing when you are on your computer?
- Do you do community service? Explain what kinds and why.
- What is a topic you know a great deal about? How did you learn this information?
- If you could have dinner with anyone alive today or from the past, who would that be? What would you discuss or what questions would you ask?
- What makes learning more enjoyable for you?
- What makes learning new information challenging?
- What else would you want me to know about you as a person? As a student and learner?

Appendix B

Checklist for Student-Led Conversations

Name____________________________________ **Date**_____________

Directions: Reflect on your role in student-led discussions. Then, use the key to mark the space at the left of each statement. Under comments, note extra details you feel are important to your self-evaluation.

KEY: N=Never S=Sometimes A=Always

PREPARATION **COMMENTS**

___Brings book and materials.
___Completes the reading.
___Helps develop discussion questions.

PARTICIPATION **COMMENTS**

___Listens without interrupting.
___Listens actively responding to peers' ideas.
___Contributes to the discussion.
___Respects different ideas and points of view.
___Recalls details to support ideas.
___Rereads a passage to support ideas.
___Asks meaningful questions.
___Keeps the discussion moving forward.

INTERPRETATION OF TEXT **COMMENTS**

___Use pictures and photos to make a point.
___Discusses literary elements offering text examples.
___Uses text features to explore meanings.
___Refers to structural elements during discussions.
___Identifies themes and main ideas in texts.
___Makes logical inferences.
___Compares and contrasts literary elements.
___Compares and contrasts information.
___Makes inter-text connections.

Additional Comments:

Appendix C

Student Observation Form

Student's Name	Monday Date:	Tuesday Date:	Wednesday Date:	Thursday Date:	Friday Date:

Appendix D

Use Literary Elements

It's easy to turn literary elements into prompts and questions to discuss fictional texts. You can introduce literary elements using the interactive read-aloud, and students can practice with narrative texts.

Antagonists: Forces that work against the protagonist and create tension in narrative texts. There are two kinds of antagonists:

- External: nature, other characters, decisions, actions taken, interactions
- Internal: thoughts within the character's mind and emotions

Climax: The moment or point of greatest intensity in the plot. Short stories usually have one climax, but novels can have small climaxes as the plot unfolds. The major climax is near the end. The climax, the highest point of the action, can deepen comprehension of plot details and also offer insights into themes.

Conflicts: Struggles or differences between opposing forces such as the protagonist and nature, two characters, the protagonist and a specific event or situation, or an internal conflict within the character. Some conflicts become problems. For example, the inner conflict of deciding whether to drive in a snowstorm leads to a problem when the person's car becomes stuck in a snowdrift on a desolate road. Observing how characters deal with inner conflicts and conflicts with other characters and/or a setting can reveal much about their personalities and the themes of the narrative. There are five kinds of conflicts:

1. Person vs. Self
2. Person vs. Society
3. Person vs. Others
4. Person vs. Fate
5. Person vs. Nature

Denouement or outcome: Events that resolve the climax in a novel, short story, drama, or narrative poem are often referred to as the outcome. Understanding outcomes of a narrative can lead to figuring out themes and central themes and deepen readers' understanding of how the plot brought them back to a feeling of normalcy.

Other characters: Observing how other characters relate to, dialogue, and interact with the protagonist can deepen readers' knowledge of all their personalities as well as the themes in a story.

Plot: Events that occur in a text and enable readers to observe characters in diverse situations. Plot supports an understanding of theme, conflicts, setting, and characters' personalities. Often referred to as rising action, the plot in a text builds from the opening of the story to a high point of interest called the climax.

Point of view: This refers to who's narrating the story.

A first-person narrator is often the protagonist, and the author uses first-person pronouns: I, me, mine, we, us, our, ours.

An objective narrator acts like an observer who sees and records information and events from a neutral perspective and uses third person pronouns: he, him, his, she, her, hers, it, its, they, them, their, theirs.

An omniscient narrator knows everything about the characters, their conflicts and problems, decisions and motivation, thoughts and feelings. Told from the third-person point of view, it uses these pronouns: he, him, his, she, her, hers, it, its, they, them, their, theirs.

Protagonist: The main character in the narrative who has problems to solve. Observing how the protagonist interacts with others, makes decisions, and tries to solve problems offers insight into this character's personality and motivations.

Problem: Something that gets in the way of a character's desire or goal and requires an action or decision to overcome, such as whether to risk diving from the high board as required by the PE teacher when you're a weak swimmer or lying to your parents about where you've been to avoid punishment. Problems require characters to figure out solutions such as having no money for food or coping after a hurricane's wind and rain destroyed part of their town. How characters tackle problems and deal with their inability to resolve some can provide readers with deep insights into personality and decision-making processes.

Setting: The time and place of the narrative. A short text can focus on one setting while longer texts have multiple settings. How characters function in and react to a setting can deepen readers' understanding of characters' motivation and personality traits.

Symbolism: A symbol is one thing that represents an idea, emotion, or concept. For example, the US (NCTE guidelines) flag symbolizes patriotism and love of country; white symbolizes purity, red symbolizes blood or love, and blue symbolizes the sky, water, bravery, and dedication. Narrative authors sometimes select objects to symbolize or represent an emotion or idea they're trying to help the reader understand.

Theme: This is a statement about people and life that the author makes with the narrative. In folk and fairytales, theme is frequently stated as a moral or lesson at the end of the story.

Appendix E

Sample Unit Plan for a Unit on Biography

Reading Genre Unit Plans for Grade 8

Genre: Biography **Theme:** Obstacles

Anchor Text: *Thurgood* by Jonah Winter, illustrated by Bryan Collier, Schwartz & Wade, 2019.

Prepare an Anchor Chart: include vocabulary and discussion questions (see pages 79–83 for more on preparing anchor charts).

Vocabulary Building: 2–3 words for each chunk of text read to students; show students multiple forms of each word and discuss them.

Unit Goals: Biographies

1. are about a person who has had impact on others, and it's written by another person.
2. can be birth to death or focus on a few significant parts of a person's life.
3. can have narrative elements.
4. cite research and other sources that the author uses.
5. can include the perspective and/or conclusions of the author that might not present an accurate picture of the person's life.

Note: Students practice these goals using the anchor text (see pages 79–83).

Estimated Number of Weeks: 6

Reading Skills and Strategies: inferring, including drawing conclusions and identifying personality traits.

Assess and Build Background Knowledge: students watch videos about their person and the historical period the person lived in.

Possible Formative Assessments: teacher observations, conferences, notebook writing, students' self-evaluations; an analytical essay, illustrated timeline of significant events, reader's theater script and presentation; dramatic monologue.

Blank Unit Plan for Developing Genre Instructional Units

Reading Genre Unit Plans for Grade:

Genre: **Theme:**

Anchor Text:

Prepare an Anchor Chart

Vocabulary Building:

Unit Goals: Develop an understanding of:

Note: Students practice these goals using the anchor text (see pages 79–83).

Genre Structure:

Estimated Number of Weeks:

Reading Skills and Strategies:

Assess and Build Background Knowledge:

Possible Formative Assessments:

Appendix F

Two Short Texts That Can Be Used as Anchor Texts

For a Unit on Realistic Fiction

Hoops Tryouts

by Anina Robb

"Brian! Breakfast!" Brian's mom was knocking at his locked bedroom door. "Why is this door locked, young man?"

"I'll be out in a second, Mom." Brian leapt down from the top bar of his bunkbed where he'd been hanging, stretching, his toes dangling, his white pajama pants flapping like a flag of surrender.

And, in fact, today, that was all that Brian wanted to do—give up. He'd been stretching from his bunk for the last month, and he was still the shortest boy in seventh grade. He was shorter than most of the girls. Heck, he was shorter than even the sixth graders. Basketball tryouts were today, and if he didn't make the team, he knew he'd disgrace his family.

"Finally," his mom sighed as Brian slid into his chair at the kitchen table. She piled a heaping serving of scrambled eggs on his plate. "Eat up. You have a big day!"

His big brother, Jonas, had already finished breakfast.

"A kiss goodbye for your mama?" their mom joked, and Jonas turned to bend down to kiss her. Then he smacked Brian on the head. Brian thought this could mean one of two things: I love you, or you are an idiot.

Jonas was a sophomore in high school and almost six feet tall. He'd been a starter on the basketball team since junior high. Everyone knew he'd get a basketball college scholarship one day. Brian shoved the eggs in his mouth.

"Alex is here. Don't forget your lunch money!" his mom called as Brian slid his plate into the sink and grabbed the coins from the bowl. Alex knocked on the screen door like a trusty alarm at 8:05. The two friends had been walking to school together since second grade, but Alex only cared about basketball because his friend liked it—he was more interested in computers.

"Ready for tryouts?"

Brian shrugged. "I guess. Ready as I'll ever be."

"What you gonna do about Lesh?"

Matt Lesh thought he was the best basketball player in seventh grade because he was five feet ten. He'd been picking on Brian for being short so long that Brian couldn't remember a time he hadn't. In fact, it was Lesh who had inspired Brian to try to stretch himself out. Of course, Brian didn't tell anyone he was trying it.

The first bell was already ringing, which meant five minutes to get to class. Brian fumbled at his locker. When he finally opened it, Matt Lesh darted around the corner and slammed his locker door shut.

"Oops, my bad!" and he was gone. Brian didn't have time to react or say anything. He had to get his locker open again so he could get to first block on time.

At lunch, things just got worse. In the lunch line, Matt was full of put-downs: "How about some shrimp, today? No, maybe a small fry? Would you like some peanuts with that?"

Brian was getting hot; he could feel his face flushing red like the roses in his grandmother's garden.

"Just ignore him, Brian." Alex elbowed his friend along in line. "He's not worth it."

After school, the gym was bustling with boys trying out for the basketball team. The coaches lined everyone up in order from tallest to shortest, and wouldn't you know? Brian was dead last.

"End of the line, eh, Brian?" Coach Peters chuckled. For a moment,
Brian thought of splitting—just hightailing it out of there and not looking back. Jeez, even the coaches were making fun of him. But he'd been practicing for weeks to get on this team, and he knew that being tall was not the end-all, be-all for junior high basketball.

Besides, he was bound to grow sometime soon, and then everyone would need someone else to sneer at.

"All right," Coach Peters boomed, "this tryout is made up of four different stations: a dribbling through cones drill, jump shooting, passing, and an agility drill. Let's pair up and get started. Front of the line—you're with the back of the line and so on!"

Brian froze. It couldn't be. This was his worst nightmare ever. He was paired with Matt Lesh.

Matt jogged over. "You better make me look good, Short Stuff."

And in that moment, Brian decided the thing to do was to make himself look good: to take all the work he had put in the last few weeks and show it off—not for Matt or his brother or his mom but for himself. He deserved a spot on this team because he was good, and he worked hard, and he was a team player. Brian took off to the first station, leaving Matt in his shadow.

"Hey, wait up!" Matt shouted, but Brian moved on.

And that is how each station went—he dribbled by Matt, he out-passed him, he threw more jump shots, and his feet were lighter on the basketball court during the agility drills.

Sweaty and hot, the boys slumped by the bleachers when the coach blew the whistle.

"All right, good work out there today. Good hustle. A team roster will be posted tomorrow morning by the gym."

As everyone started shuffling out the double doors, Brian spotted Alex waiting for him across the street. Just as he turned to slip on his jacket, there was Matt Lesh behind him. He braced himself for the coming insult. Instead Max raised his hand for a high-five. Brian reluctantly raised his, too.

"Nice." Matt nodded his head and jogged away.

"What the heck was that?" Alex asked as they fell into step together.

Brian shrugged his shoulders. Even if he didn't make the team tomorrow, he was hoping things would be different from here on out.

For a Unit on Biography

Defying Gravity: Mae Jemison

by Anina Robb

Have you ever wanted to float above the earth? Or maybe defy gravity? Dr. Mae Jemison did, but she couldn't decide how to best achieve this goal. Perhaps she should study science and become an astronaut? Or maybe she should follow her love of dance and become a professional dancer? At first glance, these two dreams seem like they belong at the opposite ends of a wish list, but Mae Jemison followed both her dreams of dancing and becoming an astronaut. She became the first African American woman astronaut and showed the world how dancing and space travel aren't that different.

Born October 17, 1956, in Decatur, Alabama, Mae and her family moved to Chicago when she was only three. Mae always considered Chicago her home. As a young girl, Mae imagined that "by now we'd be going into space like you were going to work." Her parents were always very supportive of her dreams of studying science—even if her teachers were not always so open-minded. When Mae was five years old, her kindergarten teacher asked her what she wanted to be when she grew up. Mae replied, "A scientist!"

Her teacher was surprised as there weren't many women scientists in 1961. So, her teacher said, "You must mean a nurse?"

And Mae remembers thinking that there was nothing wrong with being a nurse, but that was not what she wanted to be. So, she said, "No, a scientist!"

Mae also loved to dance. As a young girl, she took every kind of dance she could—ballet, tap, jazz, and African. Most people might think that dance is the exact opposite of science. After all, it is an art. What could dance training possibly offer to becoming a scientist or an astronaut? As Mae put it, "In dance class, I grew stronger and gained an appreciation for hard work, physical strength, and grace."

The lessons she learned from dance would eventually serve her very well in her astronaut training.

Mae graduated from high school early; she was only sixteen. At the time, she did not realize that this was an achievement. It wasn't until she arrived at the campus of Stanford University in California—far from her Chicago home—that she realized how young she was. Throughout Mae's college years, her interests remained wide and varied, not just science. At Stanford, she studied both physical and social sciences. Mae learned Russian and African languages. Her college degrees were in chemical engineering and African studies.

After college, Mae was trying to figure out what she wanted to do with her life; she was trying to decide whether to continue on to medical school at Cornell or to become a professional dancer. Like a lot of young adults, she turned to her mother for advice. Her mother told her, "You can always dance if you are a doctor, but you can't doctor if you are a dancer."

So, Mae put aside her dream of professional dancing and went on to medical school for four years and became a doctor.

The next stop on Mae's career path was the Peace Corps. She served as a medical officer in the Peace Corps from 1983 to 1985. Her main job was to care for Peace Corps volunteers serving in Liberia and Sierra Leone, Africa. It was during this time that she applied to the astronaut program at NASA. Mae was inspired to follow through on her dream of becoming an astronaut by the African American actress who played Lieutenant Uhura on the TV show *Star Trek*. She also could tell that the space program was opening up to women after the historic flight of the first American woman, Sally Ride, in 1983.

In 1987, NASA accepted Mae into its Astronaut Training Program. Only fifteen candidates were chosen that year out of over 2,000 applicants. She was part of a highly select group of trainees being groomed to fly the next shuttle into space. She trained at their facilities in Texas and in Florida and learned all about space exploration—the hard work and the physical strength needed to be an astronaut. She worked for NASA and waited for a chance to go up on one of the space shuttles.

In 1992, that chance finally came. The space shuttle *Endeavor* launched on September 12, 1992, and Mae Jemison became the first African American woman to orbit the earth. Mae has happy memories of that flight and looking out the window down onto planet Earth. She looked down from the space shuttle and saw the city of Chicago—her childhood home. She said, "I felt like I belonged right there in space. I realized I would be comfortable anywhere in the universe because I belonged to and was part of it as much as any star, planet, asteroid, comet, or nebula."

Because of her love of dance and as a salute to creativity, Mae took a poster of the Alvin Ailey American Dance Theater along with her on her historic space flight. She said, "Many people don't see the connection between science and dance, but I consider them both to be expressions of the boundless creativity that people have to share with one another."

What is it that we can take away from Mae Jemison's life experiences? It might be to never stop following your passions and dreams because we never know where they might lead us—maybe right out of this world!

Appendix G

Some Guidelines for Teaching with Informational Texts

Help students identify the text structures that are part of informational texts as well as how the structure deepens their understanding of the information presented. These six structures can also be found in narrative texts and work together. For example, description can be part of sequencing, compare/contrast, etc.

- description
- sequence
- compare/contrast
- cause/effect
- problem/solution
- question/answer

You'll also want to show students how to apply these reading strategies:

- **Inferring** by using details in the text to predict, draw conclusions, and infer or find unstated meanings.
- **Determining important ideas** by asking students to select key ideas the author presents by separating these from less important material.
- **Identifying themes** as an aspect of inferring for the implied big ideas.
- **Visualizing parts** of the text to increase understanding.
- **Comparing/contrasting** invites students to move beyond a small section of text to using a wide range of details.
- **Connecting ideas within the text** to show how they relate and strengthen or weaken information and arguments.

Appendix H

Five-Minute Conference Form

Student's Name____________________________**Date**______________

BEFORE THE CONFERENCE
Focused Topic:

Teacher's preparation notes:

AFTER THE CONFERENCE
Student's comments:

Outcomes:

Negotiated goal:

Check one:
____schedule another conference
____have the student work with a peer
____have the student work independently

Appendix I

Reading Log Form

Name: ______________________________ Date Completed / Abandoned __________

Appendix J

Develop a Thesis and Defend It

A thesis is a claim, a position that grows out of information in a text and can be defended using evidence from that text. Themes can be transformed into thesis statements, so knowing the themes in a book can help students develop a clear and compelling thesis.

For example, using the anchor text "Grandmother's Table" (see page 80), here are themes seventh graders identified:

- Age discrimination can hurt defenseless elderly men and women.
- Kindness can bring hope to others.
- One person who speaks out can change your thinking and attitude.
- A lack of empathy can spotlight insensitive behavior.

Students worked in teams and used the above list of themes to develop these thesis statements:

- Discriminating against older people with infirmities leaves them defenseless and unable to stand up for their rights and share their feelings.
- Kindness and understanding toward infirm elderly people brings hope into their lives.
- Sometimes all it takes is one person speaking the truth to change the insensitive actions of others.
- Those who lack empathy for others and so can't imagine how others feel can make decisions that result in pain and sadness.

Sample Lesson for Analytical Paragraphs

Jotting notes prior to writing asks students to do their selecting and thinking first. Having text evidence that supports a thesis offers students choices and enables them to decide whether there is enough text evidence to adequately support the thesis statement they selected.

Text: "Grandmother's Table" by the Brothers Grimm

Thesis Statement: Sometimes all it takes is one person speaking the truth to change the insensitive actions of others.

Text Evidence

- The son and his daughter took the son's mother into their home after her husband died.
- Both son and daughter were insensitive to the fact that the old woman had poor eyesight and her hands trembled, causing her to spill food over the table at meals.
- The day the old woman knocked over a glass of milk, the son and his wife had it. They moved the old woman to a table near the broom closet to eat alone and be ignored.
- When the son's daughter used her blocks to build a table for her parents when they got old, the parents came to their senses. The feelings they instantly experienced enabled them to be empathetic to the old woman.
- From that point on, everyone ate together.
- What we model for our children can often return to us.

Compose a Sample Paragraph

Collaborate with students to write the paragraph. Invite students to select three pieces of text evidence and use each one to compose sentences. Doing this can build students' mental model of the writing process. You'll most likely have to collaborate more than once until you see students' contributions to the notes and writing flow. Then, have them work with a partner if they need this support and eventually on their own.

Appendix K

Sample Collaborative Paragraph

A Change of Heart

Sometimes all it takes is one person speaking the truth to change the insensitive actions of others. That's how the little girl in the folktale "Grandmother's Table" developed compassion in her parents. Every time the grandmother spilled food on the dinner table, her son and his wife became irritated. On the day the old woman's hands trembled so badly that she knocked over a glass of milk, the son and his wife set up a separate table near the broom closet and made the grandmother eat alone. All the time, the little girl was watching how her parents treated her grandmother. One day, the son and his wife saw their daughter playing with blocks and wondered what she was building. "I'm building a little table for you and mother so you can eat in the corner someday when I get big." These words brought both parents to their senses, and from that moment on, the old woman ate with the family. The little girl's words helped develop empathy in her parents. Once they realized what would happen to them in the future, they became more understanding and recognized how insensitive they'd been to the old woman's trembling hands and poor eyesight.

Robb's Comments: I point out to students how helpful the notes are. Since the notes represent the thinking the students did, it was easy to turn them into complete sentences. I also point out that in the wrap-up, based on the decision of the son and daughter, students inferred the pair were developing empathy and understood their lack of understanding once they observed isolation during old age could happen to them.

Grading Analytical Paragraphs

You can develop a single-point rubric (see page 111–112) or, if you want to be less formal, you can develop criteria for content that might include items from the list that follows:

- Create a thesis statement and jot text details that support it.
- Include a title that prepares readers for your position or point.
- Offer three to four details to support the thesis.
- Get readers thinking beyond the thesis in the paragraph's wrap-up.

Works Cited

Professional Books

Afflerbach, Peter. *Teaching Readers (Not Reading): Moving Beyond Skills and Strategies to Reader-Focused Instruction*. The Guilford Press, 2022.

Allington, Richard L. "If They Don't Read Much, How They Ever Gonna Get Good?" *Journal of Adolescent & Adult Literacy*, vol. 21, no. 1, 1977, pp. 57–61.

———. "Intervention All Day Long: New Hope for Struggling Readers." *Voices from the Middle*, vol. 14, no. 4, 2007, pp. 7–14.

———. *What Really Matters for Struggling Readers: Designing Research-Based Programs*. Pearson, 2011.

———. "What Really Matters When Working with Struggling Readers." *The Reading Teacher*, vol. 66, no. 7, 2013, pp. 520–30.

———. "How Reading Volume Affects Both Reading Fluency and Reading Achievement." *International Electronic Journal of Elementary Education*, vol. 7, no. 1, 2014, pp. 13–26.

Allington, Richard L., and Rachael E. Gabriel. "Every Child, Every Day." *Educational Leadership*, vol. 69, no. 6, 2012, pp. 10–15.

Allington, R. L., and A. M. McGill-Franzen. "Reading Volume and Reading Achievement: A Review of Recent Research." *Reading Research Quarterly*, vol. 56, no. 1, 2021, pp. 231–38.

Anderson, Jeff, et al. *Patterns of Power, Grades 6–8: Inviting Adolescent Writers into the Conventions of Language*. Stenhouse Publishers, 2021.

Anderson, Richard C., et al. "Growth in Reading and How Children Spend Their Time Outside of School." *Reading Research Quarterly*, vol. 23, no. 3, 1988, pp. 285–303.

Atwell, Nancie. *In the Middle: A Lifetime of Learning about Writing, Reading, and Adolescents*. 3rd ed., Heinemann, 2014.

Bray, Barbara, and Kathleen McClaskey. *How to Personalize Learning: A Practical Guide for Getting Started and Going Deeper*. Corwin, 2016.

Brozo, William G., Gerry Shiel, and Keith Topping. "Engagement in Reading: Lessons Learned from Three PISA Countries." *Journal of Adolescent & Adult Literacy*, vol. 51, no. 4, 2007, pp. 304–15.

Brozo, William G., Nancy Frey, and Gay Ivey. *50 Content Area Strategies for Adolescent Literacy*. Merrill/Prentice Hall, 2006.

Burke, Jim. *The English Teacher's Companion: A Completely New Guide to Classroom, Curriculum, and the Profession*. 4th ed., Heinemann, 2012.

Carbaugh, Eric, and Kristina J. Doubet. *The Differentiated Flipped Classroom: A Practical Guide to Digital Learning*. Corwin, 2015.

Cherry-Paul, Sonja, and Dana Johansen. *Breathing New Life into Book Clubs: A Practical Guide for Teachers*. Heinemann, 2019.

"Children's Rights to Read." *International Literacy Association*, 2018, https://www.literacyworldwide.org/get-resources/childrens-rights-to-read.

Crowder, S. Travis. *Reflective Readers: The Power of Reader's Notebooks*. Benchmark Education Company, 2020.

D'Agostino, Alexa. "Students and Negotiating: Strategies That Work." *Winds of Change*, 23 Oct. 2018, https://woc.aises.org/content/students-and-negotiating-strategies-work.

Daniels, Harvey. *Literature Circles: Voice and Choice in Book Clubs and Reading Groups*. 2nd ed., Stenhouse, 2002.

———. *The Curious Classroom: 10 Structures for Teaching with Student-Directed Inquiry*. Heinemann, 2017.

DiAngelo, Robin. *White Fragility: Why It's So Hard for White People to Talk about Racism*. Beacon Press, 2018.

Dorn, Linda J., and Carla Soffos. *Teaching for Deep Comprehension: A Reading Workshop Approach*. Stenhouse Publishers, 2005.

Dweck, Carol S. *Mindset: The New Psychology of Success*. Random House, 2006.

Espana, Carla, and Luz Y. Herrera. *En Comunidad: Lessons for Centering the Voices and Experiences of Bilingual Latinx Students*. Heinemann, 2020.

Fisher, Douglas, et al. *Comprehension: The Skill, Will, and Thrill of Reading, K–12*. Corwin, 2020.

France, Paul E. *Reclaiming Personalized Learning: A Pedagogy for Restoring Equity and Humanity in Our Classrooms*. Corwin, 2019.

Friere, Paulo. *Pedagogy of the Oppressed*. 4th ed., Bloomsbury, 2018.

Garan, Elaine M., and Glenn DeVoogd. "The Benefits of Sustained Silent Reading: Scientific Research and Common Sense Converge." *Reading Teacher*, vol. 62, no. 4, 2008, pp. 336–44.

Germán, Lorena Escoto. *Textured Teaching: A Framework for Culturally Sustaining Practices*. Heinemann, 2021.

Goldberg, Gravity, and Renee Houser. *Teacher's Toolkit for Independent Reading, Grades 3 to 5*. Stenhouse Publishers, 2020.

Gonzales, Jennifer. "Know Your Terms: Holistic, Analytic, and Single-Point Rubrics." *Cult of Pedagogy,* 1 May 2014, www.cultofpedagogy.com/holistic-analytic-single-point-rubrics/.

Green Book. Directed by Peter Farrelly, Universal Pictures, 2018.

Harvey, Stephanie, and Anne Goudvis. *Strategies That Work: Teaching Comprehension for Understanding and Engagement*. 2nd ed., Pearson, 2007.

Heritage, Margaret. *Formative Assessment: Making It Happen in the Classroom.* 2nd ed., Corwin, 2021.

Hinchman, Kathleen A., and Heather K. Sheridan-Thomas. *Best Practices in Adolescent Literacy Instruction.* 3rd ed., Guilford Press, 2022.

Howard, Mary. *RTI from All Sides: What Every Teacher Needs to Know.* Heinemann, 2009.

Kay, Matthew R. *No Light, but Fire: How to Lead Meaningful Race Conversations in the Classroom.* Stenhouse Publishers, 2018.

Keene, Ellin O. *Engaging Children: Igniting a Drive for Deeper Learning*. Heinemann, 2018.

Kendi, Ibram X. *How to Be an Antiracist*. One World, 2019.

Korbey, Holly. "The Reading Wars: Choice vs. Canon." *Edutopia,* 9 July 2019, www.edutopia.org/article/reading-wars-choice-vs-canon.

Krashen, Stephen D. *The Power of Reading: Insights from the Research.* 2nd ed., Libraries Unlimited, 2004.

Lee, Laura. "Optimizing Station Rotations in Blended Learning." Edutopia, 20 Sept. 2019, www.edutopia.org/article/optimizing-station-rotations-blended-learning.

Lent, ReLeah C. *This Is Disciplinary Literacy: Reading, Writing, Thinking, and Doing…Content Area by Content Area.* Corwin, 2015.

MacKenzie, Trevor. *Dive into Inquiry: Amplify Learning and Empower Student Voice.* EdTechTeam Press, 2016.

Macon, James M., et al. *Responses to Literature: Grades K-8*. International Reading Association, 1990.

Miller, Donalyn, and Colby Sharp. *Game Changer! Book Access for All Kids.* Scholastic Professional, 2018.

Minor, Cornelius. *We Got This.: Equity, Access, and the Quest to Be Who Our Students Need Us to Be*. Heinemann, 2018.

Muhammad, Gholdy. *Cultivating Genius: An Equity Framework for Culturally and Historically Responsive Literacy.* Scholastic Teaching Resources, 2020.

Mulligan, Tammy, and Clare Landrigan. "It's All about the Books: Create Bookrooms and Classroom Libraries That Inspire Readers." Heinemann Blog, 2018, https://blog.heinemann.com/how-does-having-a-school-library-and-a-bookroom-maximize-access.

NCTE. "Statement on Independent Reading." *National Council of Teachers of English*, 7 Nov. 2019, https://ncte.org/statement/independent-reading/.

Ness, Molly, et al. "The Power of Authentic Texts: Effective Pathways to Developing a Reading Culture and Student Success." Penguin Random House, 2020.

Newkirk, Thomas. *Minds Made for Stories: How We Really Read and Write Informational and Persuasive Texts*. Heinemann, 2014.

Novak, Katie, and Catlin R. Tucker. *UDL and Blended Learning: Thriving in Flexible Learning Landscapes*. Impress, 2021.

Osorio, Sandra L. "Building Culturally and Linguistically Sustaining Spaces for Emergent Bilinguals: Using Read-Alouds to Promote Translanguaging." *The Reading Teacher*, vol. 74, no. 2, 2020, pp. 137–46.

Owocki, Gretchen. *The RTI Daily Planning Book, K–6: Tools and Strategies for Collecting and Assessing Reading Data & Targeted Follow-Up Instruction*. Heinemann, 2010.

Owocki, Gretchen, and Yetta Goodman. *Kidwatching: Documenting Children's Literacy Development*. Heinemann, 2002.

Rasinski, Timothy. *The Fluent Reader: Oral & Silent Reading Strategies for Building Fluency, Word Recognition & Comprehension*. 2nd ed., Scholastic Professional, 2020.

Rasinski, Timothy, and Melissa Cheesman Smith. *The Megabook of Fluency*. Scholastic Professional, 2018.

Reutzel, D. Ray, and Stephanie Juth. "Supporting the Development of Silent Reading Fluency: An Evidence-Based Framework for the Intermediate Grades (3–6)." *International Electronic Journal of Elementary Education*, vol. 7, no. 1, 2014, pp. 27–46, https://files.eric.ed.gov/fulltext/EJ1053594.pdf.

Ripp, Pernille. Virginia State Reading Association's Annual Conference, 2018, Norfolk, VA. Keynote Speech.

Robb, Laura. *Differentiating Reading Instruction: How to Teach Reading to Meet the Needs of Each Student*. Scholastic Teaching Resources, 2008.

———. *Vocabulary Is Comprehension: Getting to the Root of Text Complexity*. Corwin, 2014.

———. *Read, Talk, Write: 35 Lessons That Teach Students to Analyze Fiction and Nonfiction*. Corwin, 2017.

Robb, Laura, and Evan Robb. *Schools Full of Readers: Tools for Teachers, Coaches, and Leaders to Support Students*. Benchmark Education Company, 2020.

Robb, Laura, and David L. Harrison *Guided Practice for Reading Growth*. Corwin, 2020.

Robb, Laura, et al. *Differentiating Instruction for Growth in Reading*. Shell Education, 2023.

Rosenblatt, Louise. *Literature as Exploration*. 4th ed., The Modern Language Association, 1983.

Rothstein, Dan, and Luz Santana. "Teaching Students to Ask Their Own Questions." *Harvard Education Letter*, vol. 27, no. 5, 2011, pp. 1–2.

Samuels, S. Jay, and Yi-Chen Wu. "How the Amount of Time Spent on Independent Reading Affects Reading Achievement: A Response to the National Reading Panel." *CiteSeer*, Jan. 2004, http://citeseerx.ist.psu.edu/viewdoc/summary?doi=10.1.1.539.9906.

Scholastic. "Kids & Family Reading Report: 5th Edition." Scholastic, 2015, www.scholastic.com/content/dam/KFRR/PastReports/KFRR2015_5th.pdf.

———. "Teacher & Principal School Report: Focus on Literacy." Scholastic, 2017, http://mediaroom.scholastic.com/press-release/new-research-reveals-teachers-value-independent-reading-time-only-36-can-set-aside-tim.

———. "Kids & Family Reading Report: 7th Edition." Scholastic, 2019, www.scholastic com/readingreport/home.html/

Sims Bishop, Rudine. "Mirrors, Windows, and Sliding Glass Doors."*Perspectives: Choosing and Using Books for the Classroom*, vol. 6, no. 3, 1990, pp. 9–11.

Singleton, Glenn E. *Courageous Conversations about Race: A Field Guide for Achieving Equity in Schools and Beyond*. 3rd ed., Corwin, 2021.

Styslinger, Mary. "Why 'Workshop' the Canon?" National Council of Teachers of English, 4 Dec. 2017, https://ncte.org/blog/2017/12/why-workshop-the-canon/.

Tomlinson, Carol Ann. *How to Differentiate Instruction in Academically Diverse Classrooms*. 3rd ed., ASCD, 2017.

Tomlinson, Carol Ann, and Tonya R Moon. *Assessment and Student Success in a Differentiated Classroom*. ASCD, 2013.

Tucker, Catlin. *Power Up Blended Learning: A Professional Learning Infrastructure to Support Sustainable Change*. Corwin, 2018.

———. "Station Rotation in an Era of Social Distancing & Online Learning." Catlin Tucker, 21 June 2020, https://catlintucker.com/2020/06/station-rotation-in-an-era-of-social-distancing/.

Tucker, Catlin R., et al. *Blended Learning in Action: A Practical Guide toward Sustainable Change*. Corwin, 2016.

Urbanksi. Cynthia D. *Using the Workshop Approach in the High School English Classroom: Modeling Effective Writing, Reading, and Thinking Strategies for Student Success*. Skyhorse, 2015.

Vaughn, Margaret, and Dixie D. Massey. *Teaching with Children's Literature: Theory to Practice*. Guilford Press, 2021.

Wells, Gordon. *The Meaning Makers: Children Learning Language and Using Language to Learn*. Heinemann, 1985.

Wilhelm, Jeffrey, et al. *Reading Unbound: Why Kids Need to Read What They Want and Why We Should Let Them*. Scholastic Teaching Resources, 2013.

Wiliam, Dylan. *Embedded Formative Assessment*. 2nd ed., Solution Tree Press, 2017.

Zimmermann, Susan, and Ellin O. Keene. *Mosaic of Thought: The Power of Comprehension Strategy Instruction*. 2nd ed., Heinemann, 2007.

Children's Literature

Ahmed, Samira. *Internment.* Little, Brown Books for Young Readers, 2019.

Alexie, Sherman. *The Absolutely True Diary of a Part-Time Indian*. Little, Brown Books for Young Readers, 2009.

Brothers Grimm. "Grandmother's Table." *The Complete Fairy Tales of the Brothers Grimm*, Bantam, 1987.

Bruchac, Joseph. *Two Roads*. Dial Books, 2018.

Clavell, James. *The Children's Story*. Dell, 1989.

Creech, Sharon. *Love That Dog*. HarperCollins, 2001.

Dashner, James. *The Maze Runner: Book 1*. Delacorte Press, 2010.

Dickens, Charles. *A Tale of Two Cities*. Dover Publications, 1998.

———. *Captain Murderer.* Adapted by George Harland. Lothrop, Lee & Shepard Books, 1986.

Eliot, George. *Silas Marner*. Penguin Classics, 2003.

Engle, Margarita. *The Poet Slave of Cuba: A Biography of Juan Francisco Manzano.* Illustrated by Sean Qualls. Square Fish, 2011.

———. *Enchanted Air: Two Cultures, Two Wings: A Memoir*. Atheneum Books for Young Readers, 2016.

Frank, Anne. *Anne Frank: The Diary of a Young Girl.* Translated by B. M. Mooyaart. Bantam, 1993.

Goodman, Susan E. *The First Step: How One Girl Put Segregation on Trial.* Bloomsbury USA Childrens, 2016.

Grimes, Nikki. *Bronx Masquerade*. Speak, 2003.

Hawthorne, Nathaniel. *The Scarlet Letter*. Warbler Classics, 2020.

Hesse, Karen. *Witness.* Scholastic, 2003.

———. *Out of the Dust*. Scholastic, 2012.

Homer. *The Odyssey*. Penguin Classics, 1999.

Hosseini, Khaled. *The Kite Runner.* Riverhead Books, 2013.

Joseph, Frederick. *The Black Friend: On Being a Better White Person*. Candlewick, 2020.

Lai, Thanhha. *Inside Out and Back Again*. HarperCollins, 2013.

Lee, Harper. *To Kill a Mockingbird*. HarperPerennial, 2002.

Lewis, John, Andrew Aydin, and Nate Powell. *March: Book One*. Top Shelf Productions, 2013.

London, Jack. *The Call of the Wild.* Dover Publications, 1990.

Lowery, Lynda Blackmon. *Turning 15 on the Road to Freedom: My Story of the 1965 Selma Voting Rights March*. Speak, 2016.

Lowry, Lois. *The Giver*. Houghton Mifflin Harcourt, 2012.

Malamud, Bernard. "A Summer's Reading." *The Magic Barrel: Stories*. Farrar, Straus and Giroux, 2003.

Marable, Manning, and Leith Mullings. *Freedom: A Photographic History of the African American Struggle*. Phaidon Press, 2005.

Medina, Tony. *Love to Langston*. Lee & Low Books, 2006.

Morgan, Genevieve A. *The Fog of Forgetting*. Islandport Press, 2014.

———. *The Kinfolk*. Islandport Press, 2016.

Morrow, Bethany C., editor. *Take the Mic: Fictional Stories of Everyday Resistance*. Arthur A. Levine Books, 2019.

Orwell, George. *1984*. Signet Classic, 1961.

Park, Linda S. *A Long Walk to Water*. Clarion Books, 2010.

Paterson, Katherine. *The Great Gilly Hopkins*. HarperCollins, 2004.

Reynolds, Jason, and Brendan Kiely. *All American Boys*. Atheneum/Caitlyn Dlouhy Books, 2015.

Reynolds, Jason, and Ibram X. Kendi. *Stamped: Racism, Antiracism, and You*. Little, Brown Books for Young Readers, 2020.

Sánchez, Erika L. *I Am Not Your Perfect Mexican Daughter*. Knopf, 2017.

Shakespeare, William. *Romeo and Juliet*. Simon & Schuster, 2004.

———. *Julius Caesar*. Simon & Schuster, 2004.

Sleator, William. "The Elevator." *Things That Go Bump in the Night*, edited by Jane Yolen, HarperCollins, 1989.

Soto, Gary. "Seventh Grade." *Baseball in April and Other Stories*. Houghton Mifflin Harcourt, 2000.

Steinbeck, John. *Of Mice and Men*. Penguin Classics, 1993.

———. *The Pearl*. Penguin Classics, 2000.

Stevenson, Robert Louis. *Treasure Island*. Penguin Classics, 1999.

Stine, R. L. "I'm Not Martin." *Nightmare Hour: Time for Terror*. HarperCollins, 2020.

Stone, Nic. *Clean Getaway*. Crown Books for Young Readers, 2020.

———. *Dear Martin*. Crown Books for Young Readers, 2017.

Takei, George, et al. *They Called Us Enemy*. Top Shelf Productions, 2019.

Taylor, Mildred. *The Friendship*. Puffin Books, 1998.

Thomas, Angie. *The Hate U Give*. Blazer + Bray, 2017.

Twain, Mark. *Adventures of Huckleberry Finn*. Dover Publications, 1994.

Weatherford, Carole Boston. *Freedom on the Menu: The Greensboro Sit-Ins*. Illustrated by Jerome Lagarrigue, Dial Books, 2004.

Winter, Jonah. *Thurgood*. Illustrated by Bryan Collier, Schwartz & Wade, 2019.

Woodson, Jacqueline. *Each Kindness*. Nancy Paulsen Books, 2012.

Zoboi, Ibi, and Yusef Salaam. *Punching the Air*. HarperCollins, 2020.

Index

The letter *f* following a page locator denotes a figure.

access, defined, 18
achievement, reading and, 8
agency, engagement and, 5
Allington, Richard, 9, 118
anchor text lessons, 79–83
anchor texts, sample, 133–137
Anderson, Richard C., 8
antagonists, defined, 128
antiracist, defined, 18
assessment. *See also* grading; self-assessment
  authentic, 119
  book reviews for, 48–50, 51–53*f*
  book shares for, 44
  book talks for, 44–47, 46*f*
  book trailers for, 48
  conferences for, 96, 98
  eliminating, 42–43
  enjoyable, 44
  formative, xv, 67–71, 69*f*
  of independent reading, 42–50, 45*f*, 51–53*f*
  peer book conferences for, 44, 45*f*
  planning for, 94
  readers' notebooks for, 110
  rubrics for, 94–96, 97
  of small-group learning, 65–71, 66*f*, 69*f*
  student-led literary conversations for, 65, 66*f*
asset model, xv
attitude-volume relation, 7
Atwell, Nancie, 8

background knowledge, building, xv, 35–36
"Become a Reading Principal" (Robb), 31–32
Bishop, Rudine Sims, 21–22
Black Lives Matter movement, 16
blended learning, 30
book clubs, 54, 57–58, 121
book conferences, peer for assessment, 44, 45*f*
book discussions
  notebook writing after, 91–93
  online, 27–28
book reports, eliminating, 42
book reviews for assessment, 48–50, 51–53*f*
book talks, 44–48, 46*f*
book trailers, 48
Brozo, William, 6

characters, other, 129
choice, engagement and, 4–5
classroom libraries. *See also* core collections
  assessing to get started, 119
  culturally relevant, 39–40
  evaluating and choosing texts for, 24–25, 40
  genre organization, 40
  to support volume reading, 9–10
  vignette, 2–3

climax, defined, 128
communication, engagement and honest, 6
comprehension, improving, xv
conferences
  for assessment, 109–110
  enjoyable, 96, 98
  Five-Minute Conference Form, 139
  peer book conferences, 44, 45*f*
conflicts
  defined, 128
  discussion using, 78
conversations
  Fishbowl Conversation (activity), 62–63
  on racism and white privilege, texts for, 25–27
  student-led, checklist for, 126
  student-led literary, 61–62, 63–67, 66*f*
core collections. *See also* classroom libraries
  assessment options, 108
  benefits of using, 101, 116
  culturally relevant, 105–107
  high school sample units, 114–116
  middle school sample units, 113–114
  planning units with, 112–113
  reading the world through, 116–117
  students' notebook writing on, 107–109
core texts
  choosing related texts, 101–102
  four words response, 104–105
  modeling notebook writing about, 104–105
  modeling thinking about and analyzing, 103–104
  organizing, 102–103
  purpose of, 100
  teachers' notebooks on, 104
  themes from, 100–101
cultural relevance
  classroom libraries, 39–40
  core collections, 105–107
  texts with, 21–25, 105–107
curriculum, culturally relevant texts in the, 21–25
decision-making, negotiation in student, 56–57
decoding, practicing, xv
deficit model, defined, 18
denouement, defined, 128–129
dioramas, eliminating, 42
disciplinary literacy, 121–122
discussion. *See also* book discussions
  independent reading supporting, 37–38
  instructional unit teaching tools, 84, 86–87, 91–93
  literary elements for, 128–130
  methods of, 77–79
  of racism and white privilege, 25–27

engagement
  elements of, 4–6
  importance of, 1–3
  relevance and, 100
  volume and, 6–7
"Engagement in Reading: Lessons Learned from Three PISA Countries" (Brozo, Shiel, & Topping), 6
Engaging Children: Igniting a Drive for Deeper Learning K-8 (Keene), 7
equity, defined, 18

fiction summarizing, discussion using, 78
Fishbowl Conversation (activity), 62–63
Five-Minute Conference Form, 139
flipped learning, 30
Floyd, George, 16
fluency, independent reading supporting, 37
formative assessment
  asset model of, xv
  observation for, 68, 69*f*, 70–71
four words response, 104–105
Friere, Paolo, 16–17

genre instructional library, 74–75
genre questions, discussion using, 77
genre structure, independent reading supporting, 37
Giles, Lamar, 21
grading. *See also* assessment

analytical paragraphs, 143–144
student-led literary conversations, 65, 66*f*
students' notebooks, 90
Graves, Donald, 14
growth mindset, 5

homework, writing about and posting, 12
hybrid learning, 30

independent reading
assessment of, 42–50, 45*f*, 51–53*f*
benefits of, 40–41
foundational skills supported by, 35–38
frequency-volume relation, 6
NCTE position statement on, 10
independent reading of self-selected books
benefits of, 10–11
engagement and, 4–5
monitoring, 29
relevance through, 28–29
informational texts, teaching with, 138
instructional unit libraries, 73–76
instructional unit reading
assessment rubrics, 94–96
benefits of, 11
managing, 84–85
planning for with core collections, 112–113
sample unit plan for a unit on biography, 131–132
self-assessment, 96
instructional units
student partnerships during, 76–77
instructional units, teaching tools
anchor text lessons, 79–83
book discussions, 91–93
halfway point, 87
note-taking for summarizing, 85–86
partner discussions, 84, 86–87
second books and beyond, 87
students' notebooks, 88–93
teachers' notebooks, 87–88
intentionality
in changing bad policies, 18–19
teaching with, 16–17
interest inventories, 38–39, 125
"Intervention All Day Long: New Hope for Struggling Readers" (Allington), 118

Keene, Ellin, 7
Kendi, Ibram X., 17

Lao Tzu, 19
leisure reading, engagement and, 6
libraries. *See also* classroom libraries; instructional unit libraries
culturally relevant, 39–40
evaluating and choosing texts for, 24–25, 40
organizing, 39–40, 73
storage needs, 75–76
literacy, defined, 6
literary elements, discussion using, 78, 128–130
Love, Bettina, 21

media centers, 11–12

nonfiction summarizing, discussion using, 79
notebooks
housing, 12
purpose of, 12, 88
students,' 88–93
teachers,' 87–88
notebook writing
after book discussions, 91–93
for assessment, 110
on core collections, 107–109
examples, 89*f*, 91–93*f*
modeling, 104–105, 120
responding to, 90
of summaries, eliminating, 43

observation
for formative assessment, 68, 69*f*, 70–71
moving forward through, 120

Observation Form, 127
outcome, defined, 128–129
ownership, agency and, 5

paragraphs
  sample, 142
  sample collaborative, 143–144
parent signatures, eliminating, 43
Pedagogy of the Oppressed (Friere), 16–17
peer book conferences, 44, 45*f*
personalized learning, 29–30
plot, defined, 129
point of view, defined, 129
principal, becoming a reading, 31–32
problem, defined, 129
protagonist, defined, 129

questions
  closed, 61–62
  guiding, 61
  open-ended interpretive, 58, 61–62

racial inequities, defined, 18
racism
  books to start conversations about, 25–27
  commitment to ending, 18–21
  texts on, 21, 22
racist, defined, 18
Rasinski, Timothy, 37
read-alouds
  daily, benefits of, 12–13
  for diversity, cultural relevance, inclusion, 23
  required, 99
readers' theater scripts, 60–61
reading groups, teacher-led, 59–60
Reading Log Form, 43, 140
reflection, engagement and, 6
relationships. *See* teacher-student relationships
relevance, creating, 28–29
relevance-engagement relation, 100
rubrics
  instructional unit reading assessment, 94–96, 97
  single-point, assessment with, 111–112, 112*f*

safety
  communication and, 6
  creating an atmosphere of, xiv
  engagement and, 5–6
Samuels, S. Jay, 35
sanctuary, engagement and, 5–6
Santayana, George, 22
Schaull, Ricahrd, 17
science, reading alternate texts in, 11
self-assessment
  instructional unit reading, 96
  notebook writing, 110–111
  student-led literary conversations, 66*f*
setting, defined, 129
Shiel, Gerry, 6
silent reading, 38
Sixty-Second Elevator Talk, 10
small-group learning
  book clubs, 57–58
  class schedule, 54–56, 55*f*
  Fishbowl Conversation (activity), 62–63
  interventions, 67–68, 71
  open-ended questions in, 58, 61–62
  readers' theater scripts, 60–61
  student-led literary conversations, 61–62, 63–67, 66*f*
  teacher-led reading groups, 59–60
small-group learning assessments
  formative, 67–68, 69*f*, 70–71
  student-led literary conversations, 65, 66*f*
social studies, reading alternate texts in, 11
station learning, 30
Stone, Nic, 21
stories and storying, 1
structural racism, defined, 18
student-led literary conversations, 65, 66*f*, 126
student partnerships
  advantages, 76
  for book conferences, 44, 45*f*

in instructional units, 76–77, 84–87
organizing, 76–77
partner discussions, 84, 86–87
summaries in notebooks, eliminating, 43
symbolism, defined, 130

teachers' notebooks as teaching tools, 87–88
teachers personal reading life, importance of, 13–14
teacher-student relationships
conferences, 96, 98
engagement and, 5
know students as readers, 28
negotiation in, 56–57
one-on-one meetings, 27
share your stories, 27
small group meetings, 27–28
teaching
culturally responsive and relevant, 5, 18–25
with intentionality, 16–17
technology, learning and, 29–30
texts
culturally relevant and inclusive, 21–25, 105–107
discussion methods, 77–79
diversity-engagement relation, 6
evaluating and choosing, 24–25
informational, teaching with, 138
on racism, examples of, 21, 22
read-aloud, 99
text sets, culturally responsive and relevant, 23–24
thematic questions, discussion using, 78
theme, defined, 130
thesis defense, 141–142
time
available for reading, 3–4
spent on reading, 8, *9f*
strategic use of, xv
Topping, Keith, 6
trust, engagement and, 5

virtual/hybrid learning, 27–28
vocabulary, building, xv, 36–37
volume
Allington on, 118
importance of, 8–13
percentile rankings, minutes/day, *9f*
reasons to increase, xv
research on, 4, 6
volume, getting started with teaching for
assessment, 119
assess the classroom library, 119
content teachers, 122–123
ELA teachers, 119–122
modeling choosing good fit books, 119
reading logs for, 119
scheduling, 119
timelines, setting reasonable, 119
volume, moving forward with teaching for
adding instructional units, 120, 121
anchor texts, practice planning and teaching, 120
book clubs, introducing, 121
conferences in, 120
content subjects, 121–122
ELA teachers, 120–121
modeling notebook writing, 120
observation in, 120
self-assessment, introducing, 121
student groups, organizing, 121

white privilege, 18, 25–27
world, reading the, 116–117
writing summaries, discussion using, 78
Wu, Yi-Chen, 35

Zoboi, Ibi, 21

Author

Laura Robb is the author of several bestselling books, including *Teaching Reading in Middle School* and *Read, Talk, Write*. A teacher, coach, and consultant with more than forty years of experience in the classroom, Robb leads workshops, speaks at conferences, and coaches teachers in reading and writing around the country. A recipient of several awards for her work in literacy, Robb received NCTE's Richard Halle Award for Outstanding Middle Level Educator. She writes articles for education journals, is a regular contributor to www.therobbreviewblog.com, and has a series of podcasts with Evan Robb available at https://therobbreviewpodcast.podbean.com.

This book was typeset in TheMix and Palatino by Barbara Frazier.

Typefaces used on the cover include Balboa Condensed, and Avenir Next Demibold and Demibold Italic.

The book was printed on 50-lb. white offset paper by Sheridan.